REPORT OF THE U.S.–JAPAN STUDY GROUP
ON ARMS CONTROL AND NON-PROLIFERATION
AFTER THE COLD WAR

NEXT STEPS IN ARMS CONTROL AND NON-PROLIFERATION

Edited by William Clark, Jr., and Ryukichi Imai

CO-SPONSORED BY
CARNEGIE ENDOWMENT FOR INTERNATIONAL PEACE
INTERNATIONAL HOUSE OF JAPAN

Next Steps in Arms Control and Non-Proliferation:
Report of the U.S.–Japan Study Group on
Arms Control and Non-Proliferation After the Cold War
may be ordered ($14.95) from Carnegie's distributor,
The Brookings Institution Press, Department 029,
Washington, D.C. 20042-0029, USA.
Tel. 1-800-275-1447 or 202-797-6258. Fax 202 797-6004.

Library of Congress Cataloging-in-Publication Data
Carnegie Endowment/U.S.–Japan Study Group on
Arms Control and Non-Proliferation After the Cold War
NEXT STEPS IN ARMS CONTROL AND NON-PROLIFERATION:
Report of the U.S.–Japan Study Group on Arms Control and
Non-Proliferation After the Cold War
Editors: William Clark, Jr., and Ryukichi Imai
ISBN: 0-87003-105-8

The Carnegie Endowment for International Peace normally does not take institutional positions on public policy issues; the views and recommendations presented in this publication do not necessarily represent the views of the Carnegie Endowment or the International House of Japan, or of their officers, trustees, or staff.

CONTENTS

REPORT OF THE U.S.–JAPAN STUDY GROUP ON ARMS CONTROL AND NON-PROLIFERATION AFTER THE COLD WAR

MEMBERS OF THE STUDY GROUP

OVERVIEW: NARROWING THE GAP

WILLIAM CLARK, JR.
RYUKICHI IMAI

OVERVIEW:
NARROWING THE GAP

WILLIAM CLARK, JR.
RYUKICHI IMAI

INTRODUCTION

This is the second and final report of a two-year Japanese-American dialogue on arms control and non-proliferation issues at the global level and in East Asia. The project was co-sponsored by the Carnegie Endowment for International Peace and the International House of Japan, with the support of the United States–Japan Foundation and the Japan Foundation Center for Global Partnership.

The release of our first report, *The United States, Japan, and the Future of Nuclear Weapons*, in March 1995 occurred prior to many of the year's more significant developments in the area of nuclear non-proliferation. Indeed, it was difficult to resist the urge to anticipate the course of events in the near future while deliberating over the second half of the project agenda. This final report is an attempt at both hindsight and prescience. It presents the papers prepared by the 13 American and 13 Japanese members for the final meeting of the Study Group on September 28, 29, and 30, 1995, together with accounts of the Group's discussions on key policy issues confronting both countries.

With regard to methodology, the first three meetings of the Study Group consisted solely of full plenary sessions. However, it became apparent that time restrictions imposed by the plenary format limited discussion among the Group's members. Therefore, on the first day of the final meeting, participants were divided into four separate working groups, each of which had an American and a Japanese co-chairman and was responsible for exploring a particular topic:

Working group I:	Security and Arms Control in Asia
Working group II:	Asian Energy Development and Non-Proliferation
Working group III:	The Future of Nuclear Forces
Working group IV:	The Non-Proliferation Regime

Each of the four working groups reviewed papers focused on selected topics within its purview and attempted to arrive at agreed conclusions and recommendations. This change in format fostered more effective communication and understanding among members and between working groups. On the second full day of the conference, the four working groups presented their reports to plenary sessions in the morning and early afternoon, followed by discussion. The final plenary later in the day covered the full scope of the conference. To take into account the plenary session discussions, the working group reports were modified and are presented in each of the four sections of this book, preceding the working papers.[1]

A CHANGING ENVIRONMENT

Several pivotal events occurred between the publication of the Study Group's first report and the final deliberations in Tokyo that led to this concluding report. The most important developments were:

- The indefinite extension of the Non-Proliferation Treaty,
- The resumption of nuclear testing by France and China, and
- The signing of the Agreed Framework with North Korea.

On the whole, the global nuclear scale remained tipped toward non-proliferation and stability. However, the events of 1995 failed to demonstrate "rapid progress toward a nuclear-free world in which the need for U.S. nuclear protection would gradually decline"[2]—an objective that remains central to both U.S. and Japanese policy.

The Indefinite Extension of the Non-Proliferation Treaty

March 5, 1995, marked the 25th anniversary of the Nuclear Non-Proliferation Treaty (NPT). A full celebration had to be postponed, as the fate of the NPT, due to expire in the very same year, was determined by the NPT Review and Extension Conference held six weeks later in New York City. The indefinite and unconditional extension of the Treaty was at the top of the global arms control agenda. The NPT has the largest number of parties to any single arms control and disarmament agreement. In 1990, at the start of the fourth NPT review conference, there were 142 signatories. China and France adhered to the NPT in 1992. By the beginning of 1995, there were a total of 178 signatories.

As noted in the Study Group's initial report, the debate pitted countries favoring indefinite, unconditional extension against those advocating a variety of alternative positions, ranging from extension for limited periods to extension conditioned on steps to fulfill the Article VI obligations of nuclear powers to eliminate their nuclear weapons. In his remarks before the conference, the U.S. Secretary of State sought to reassure those opposed to indefinite extension by stating, "[t]he purpose of the NPT is to preserve the security of all, not the nuclear weapons monopoly of a few."[3] On May 11, 1995, the Review and Extension Conference decided to extend the NPT indefinitely—a decision supported by 174 signatories. Moreover, the Conference agreed to adopt a set of principles and objectives on non-proliferation and to create an enhanced review process.

The Resumption of Nuclear Testing by China and France

On May 15, 1995—just days after the Conference decided to extend the NPT indefinitely—the People's Republic of China carried out its 42nd nuclear test, disregarding the adverse impact of this poor timing on world public opinion. China explained that its decision to resume testing was based on the need to act before the Comprehensive Test Ban Treaty (CTBT) takes effect in 1996. China's subsequent decision, at the end of the month, to test-fire an intercontinental ballistic missile with an estimated range of 8,000 kilometers and a payload of 200-300 kilotons greatly heightened security concerns in the region and around the globe.[4]

Despite worldwide protest, the newly elected French President, Jacques Chirac, ended France's three-year nuclear testing moratorium by announcing plans to proceed with a series of nuclear explosions in the South Pacific at Muruora atoll. This decision provoked strong protest from Australia, New Zealand, Japan, and South Pacific nations. The 50th anniversary of the atomic bombings of Hiroshima and Nagasaki in August gave the protests further momentum. France nevertheless proceeded with its first test on September 5, 1995, despite concern that the testing violated the South Pacific Nuclear-Free Zone (SPNFZ), which had been established after earlier French testing in 1984 had led to the Treaty of Rarotonga. France promised to sign the CTBT and to comply with the SPNFZ following its planned series of tests.

On September 17, 1995, in the wake of the first French nuclear blast, the United States informed South Pacific leaders of its intent to sign the Treaty of Rarotonga and to adhere to the SPNFZ. This decision received great attention in Asia. For the preceding ten years, U.S. policy had been to abide by the terms of the Treaty, but not to accede to it. In October, France and Great Britain joined the United States in signing the Treaty. In December, however, the United States refused to sign a protocol supporting the Southeast Asian Nuclear Free Zone (SEANFZ) treaty adopted by ten southeast Asian nations. The United States objected that the treaty would not permit free transit for nuclear-armed or powered American vessels.

The Signing of the Agreed Framework with North Korea

During its first year, the Study Group conducted its meetings before the final stage of the negotiations between the United States and North Korea that resulted in the Agreed Framework of October 21, 1994. For this reason, while the majority of the Study Group's members "welcomed the agreement in the belief that its benefits outweighed its limitations and risks," the Group did not examine it in depth in its first report.

The Agreed Framework provides for a series of reciprocal actions, divided into five separate stages, that are to be completed over the course of nine years. The key concession by North Korea was its pledge to suspend its nuclear program and to allow inspectors to monitor the freeze. In return for North Korea's shutdown and the eventual dismantlement of its 5-megawatt reactor at Yongbyon, as well as termination of the construction of its 50-megawatt and 200-megawatt reactors, the United States agreed to finance the construction of two light-water reactors with a generating capacity of 2,000 megawatts. During the construction period, it agreed to provide shipments of heavy oil for heating and electricity generation rising to a level of 500,000 tons per year beginning in 1996. The Agreed Framework did not resolve the issue of whether North Korea had extracted enough plutonium from spent-fuel rods to develop nuclear weapons. Although South Korea and Japan supported the Agreed Framework and agreed to help finance it, critics in both countries objected to the fact that it did not provide for the full inspection of the North Korean nuclear program.

On November 18, 1994, Pyongyang announced that it had ceased operations at its existing 5-megawatt reactor and had suspended construction on the other two reactors. Four months later, the United States, South Korea, and Japan formally established a consortium known as the Korean Peninsula Energy Development Organization (KEDO) to organize the financing and construction of the new reactors promised to North Korea. Australia, Great Britain, New Zealand, and Singapore soon joined the original three. China proved the biggest disappointment, refusing to participate in KEDO. The financial burden fell primarily on the shoulders of South Korea, which agreed to cover the lion's share of the anticipated $4 billion cost of the two reactors, with Japan providing a significant but smaller share. The United States agreed to provide roughly $30 million per year to finance KEDO's administrative expenses, the initial shipments of heavy oil, and the costs of storing the spent-fuel rods from the Yongbyon reactor. The issue of who would pay for the bulk of the heavy oil was left unresolved.

The Agreed Framework provided for the conclusion of a contract covering construction of the two light-water reactors by April 21, 1995.

However, North Korea's initial reluctance to accept KEDO as its contractual partner and its refusal to accept South Korean reactors proved a major diplomatic hurdle. In May, the United States and North Korea negotiated a compromise on these two issues that paved the way for the conclusion of a contract between KEDO and Pyongyang in November 1995.

Although the Agreed Framework envisaged closer relations and the normalization of relations between Washington and Pyongyang, North Korean objections to the continued U.S. imposition of economic sanctions, American concerns about North Korean missile exports, and an impasse over how to replace the 1953 Armistice were among numerous issues that divided the two countries in early 1996.

KEY ISSUES

In this overview, we focus on the major themes developed in discussions in both the working groups and in the full plenary sessions. Particular emphasis has been placed on differences, in both opinion and approach, between U.S. and Japanese Study Group members. For an in-depth review of the various issues addressed by the particular working groups, the reader is directed to the papers and working group reports that follow.

In the course of our two-year study, a significant shift took place with regard to security perceptions in the region. During the 1994 meetings, much of the discussion on East Asia was centered around how to manage the growing threat from North Korea. In our 1995 meetings, the focus moved away from analyzing the security posture of the Pyongyang regime. This change has been attributable largely to the United States–North Korea Agreed Framework and to recent reports of severe economic crisis in the North. In terms of regional peace and stability, much of the Study Group's attention in 1995 focused on the direction in which China is asserting itself as it enters the next century, and on the strategic impact this will have in the region and on the United States–Japan security alliance.

Nuclear Umbrellas, Theater Missile Defense, and China

With regard to security in Asia, the Study Group spent much of its time debating the degree to which China is a threat. Many, but not all, on the American side seemed to have acknowledged China's military superiority over Japan. These American members tended to frame their arguments in terms of global imperatives relating to China, discounting specifically Japanese concerns. A majority on the Japanese side started from a very Japan-centered approach to security problems in Asia and were unwilling to relegate Japan to an inferior position vis à vis China. While acknowledging the global implications of certain policy positions relating to China, they continued to give priority to regional over global factors. Unless the differences reflected in these discussions are at least understood, if not resolved, Japanese and American policy approaches may well begin to diverge. This perceptual gap was apparent in the discussion of the future of the U.S. nuclear umbrella and the related issues of theater missile defense and global and regional arms control.

American participants attempted to allay the Japanese concern that American commitments to reduce nuclear weapons and curtail their use would lead to the withdrawal of the U.S. nuclear umbrella. The American argument was that there are two types of umbrellas. Type A was developed for Europe and can be applied to the Korean Peninsula: it refers to the first use of nuclear weapons to counter an overwhelming conventional assault. Type B refers to cases when nuclear weapons are the principal option to deter first use by another nuclear power—or are used to protect allies in the event of a nuclear attack. Type B, it was argued, applies in the case of Japan and will remain valid until nuclear weapons no longer exist.

Most American participants strongly contested Japanese suggestions that the U.S. nuclear umbrella is unreliable. In this connection, the impact of the projected Comprehensive Test Ban Treaty was examined carefully. It was agreed that no real dispute existed in Japan over whether the physical reliability of the nuclear stockpile could be maintained in the absence of testing.

Much of the debate centered on the basic question of "what is the nature of the threat?" It was asserted that, since Asia has never decoupled nuclear umbrella Type A from Type B, this has led to concern over whether the nuclear umbrella will remain effective when faced with a regional threat. With respect to Theater Missile Defense (TMD), there was division among American members, with a minority viewing it as a very hazardous development. Some argued that, because the Chinese security threat has not changed significantly, TMD ushers in a whole new era with far-reaching consequences. Given the great concern voiced over continued Chinese nuclear testing, many thought TMD development should be secondary to the goal of getting the CTBT completed in 1996. Many on both sides of the Study Group found Chinese thinking with regard to TMD approaching a double standard, i.e., that China's nuclear weapons modernization is non-threatening because of its defensive orientation, while Japan's introduction of TMD would be offensive.

In response to the view that TMD will be destabilizing if deployed, many argued that such logic is flawed with respect to Japan. The presumption that China would build up militarily to keep Japan in check was not questioned. Many argued strongly that it is morally wrong to grant China the right to target Japanese cities, but to forbid Japan to defend itself against such a threat. Others pointed out that Japanese interest in TMD is interpreted by the Chinese as stoking Japanese militarism.

Official government-to-government discussions have continued for some time between the United States and Japan over the feasibility of a TMD system. The talks have now focused on the types of threats that would be targets of TMD. Japanese participants saw their government as having an immediate and discrete need to look at TMD, but believed it was still too soon to make a decision. From the Japanese perspective, the main problems are political, fiscal, and technological in nature. Can huge cost outlays for TMD be justified politically in Japan? TMD would force a bureaucratic reorganization of the Japanese military. The cost effectiveness of the TMD system would have to be analyzed. It was thought that many in Japan would argue: if the U.S. nuclear umbrella is still valid, TMD is unnecessary. Since TMD applies to long-range missiles, the Japanese public would not support such a costly system without a pronounced nuclear threat.

There are, of course, regional concerns, other than those of China, over Japan's TMD plans. In response to such concerns, it was argued that TMD also protects against the delivery of non-nuclear weapons. Thus a Japan with TMD would be less likely to resort to nuclear weapons to counter a conventional threat. Moreover, if the Japanese government rejects TMD outright, the rest of Asia may become alarmed and interpret this as leaving Japan with only the nuclear option.

A persistent Japanese theme was that those in Japan and elsewhere who ask Japan to forego TMD are in effect asking it to remain vulnerable to China. Some members saw this question as moot—arguing that the best way to eliminate a nuclear threat is to eliminate the weapons. They posited that Japan should adopt a new policy position, similar to the Australian government's: that all nuclear weapons are illegitimate. The NPT did not legitimize the right to keep nuclear arms indefinitely, but instead recognized that five countries have them, and the norm is to move toward total elimination of such weapons. Clearly some members of the group did feel Japan should be prepared to accept lower levels of security to avoid an inevitable arms race that it could only lose.

Within Japan's current rationale for TMD, the threat from Chinese short-range missiles is perceived as less urgent than that from North Korea, considering that China has other military options. In an era when a single SS-20 missile could destroy the entire Kanto Plain, the U.S. nuclear umbrella was the only option against the Soviet threat. Today, Japan faces both a China that has developed more accurate and deadly arms and a North Korea with growing missile capabilities. When compared with current Japanese perceptions about Chinese nuclear capabilities, the Soviet arsenal now seems to have been almost invisible at the height of the Cold War.

Although long-term denuclearization is strongly supported by Japan, it would not be realistic to try to convince Japan to hold off on TMD until total nuclear disarmament is achieved. None of the Study Group participants believed that Japan's abandonment of TMD would convince China to give up or reduce its nuclear weapons. China continues to argue that, as long as Japan remains under the U.S. nuclear umbrella, criticism of China's nuclear policies by Japan is undeserved. How can Japan convince China to denuclearize?

Japan has been asked by the United States and others to help push forward the CTBT, but it was agreed that this in itself would not be enough to affect China's nuclear posture in the absence of broader global movement toward nuclear disarmament. Nevertheless, there was agreement that Japan should support global and regional denuclearization efforts while remaining under the U.S. nuclear umbrella. Most important, Japan should maintain this posture until those countries which are capable of striking Japan no longer possess nuclear arms.

The Group discussed Japan's decision to reduce its development aid to China in light of its renewed nuclear testing. Japanese members noted that aid funds are supplied by Japanese taxpayers and that the decision reflected domestic political sentiment. Many American members suggested that, in the long term, engagement was the best option to bring China closer to Japan's stance on the testing issue. The Group recognized that China remains wary of multilateral regimes related to nuclear policy and agreed that China needs to be convinced of the utility of joining with other Asian nations in the reduction, control, and non-proliferation of nuclear weapons.

If China's ultimate objective is nuclear parity with the United States and Russia, a Japanese member observed, it will be some time before China is fully cooperative, since it currently has only about 300 nuclear weapons. Several American members suggested that reducing U.S. and Russian nuclear weapons would be the best way to discourage the unlimited expansion of Chinese nuclear forces. In assessing Chinese nuclear plans, many members, both American and Japanese, felt that the emphasis on total warheads was misplaced. China's policy is focused on developing a retaliatory inventory of nuclear arms as an effective nuclear response should it come under attack, it was argued, and this has led to China's continued delay with regard to the CTBT. Japan should therefore continue engaging China, in a low-key manner, on the issue of CTBT. Given Chinese concern over TMD, in this view, the CTBT and implementation of Article VI of the NPT are both critical for stability in the region.

Although some members felt that withholding development aid was justified, it was generally agreed that such a step would fail to capture China's attention a second time. Many in the Group felt that the United States and Japan should focus instead on when, how, and under what circumstances China could be drawn into multilateral security dialogues and nuclear disarmament talks. The Group reaffirmed the 1994 Study Group recommendation that U.S.–Russian negotiations of START III (the Strategic Arms Reduction Treaty) should be accompanied by parallel discussions involving all five nuclear powers to stabilize Chinese, British, and French nuclear arsenals while the U.S.–Russian build-down proceeds and to map further reductions in the direction of zero.

Regional Impact of Nuclear Energy Development

The Japanese government has long maintained that the likelihood of using reactor-grade materials in weapons is extremely low, and it does not believe its use of plutonium to be destabilizing. On these two points, however, there were some differences among Japanese members of the Study Group and between Japanese and American members. Many Americans in the Group, in particular, felt a strong need for Japan to examine seriously the security impact of its nuclear program on other states in the Asian region.

Although the inherent disadvantages of reactor-grade plutonium for military use are often cited as making it an unlikely first option to be used by a country intent on developing nuclear weapons, both Japanese and American members of the Group identified two cases in which this argument would be irrelevant: (1) threshold states seeking to produce weapons as quickly as possible with what is on hand; and (2) sub-national groups (e.g., terrorists and rogue states) willing to work with reactor-grade plutonium because it is the easiest material to obtain.

The Group minimized the danger of terrorists acquiring reactor-grade plutonium but felt that reprocessing capabilities in the hands of rogue states could lead to breakout. For example, the Iraqis used highly enriched uranium in their reactors. Plutonium reprocessing would have allowed them to fully develop their military nuclear capabilities. More important, the development of breeder reactors would give such states high-purity, super-grade plutonium with a direct utility for nuclear weapons.

While both American and Japanese members recognized that a civilian nuclear-power program could be misused for military purposes, several Japanese members found it ironic that concern over such misuse should be voiced primarily by nuclear-weapon states that were unwilling to give up their nuclear weapons. A Japanese member of the Study Group pointedly asked, "Given that inequality is built into the NPT, why is there so much concern over plutonium issues?"

The Study Group recognized that, with the growing use of nuclear power in East Asia, Asia is the principal area where a deeper regional dialogue on nuclear issues needs to be fostered. The idea of starting a regional nuclear energy organization—an ASIATOM (Asian Atomic Energy Community)—was seen as both timely and necessary. Such a grouping could promote transparency, the safe operation of nuclear facilities, the safe disposal of nuclear waste material, and the coordinated management and inspection of plutonium and uranium stocks held by member states, including Japan. Fuel storage was discussed as a possible first topic for initiating discussions on a regional approach toward fuel-cycle issues. The Group felt that it would be premature to discuss proposals for regional reprocessing facilities and other controversial issues until the organization is well established and its scope defined.

The Study Group saw the development of the ASIATOM concept as closely linked to the security environment in Asia. The proposed start of ASIATOM comes during a period when multilateral security regimes are increasingly seen by many as the preferred regional option, leading to eventual replacement of the current bilateral alliances. Ironically, this may not bode well for the future of an ASIATOM. The U.S.–Japan security agreement currently protects only Japan, while the U.S.–Republic of Korea agreement applies strictly to South Korea. Therefore the United States may resist further multilateralization in any new effort that could have even a tangential impact on the existing security regime. In any event, the Group unanimously agreed that Chinese participation in a newly formed ASIATOM would be vital, even though China's aggressive policy stance toward Taiwan, a significant nuclear energy consumer, could complicate the issue of Chinese participation.

Two years of discussion and debate in the Study Group have narrowed the differences between the two sides regarding the military utility of reactor-grade plutonium. There is still a gap, however, in the appreciation of the perceptions of other states in the region on this subject. It does appear possible, in the ASIATOM context, that these differences can be resolved in the not too distant future.

Prospects for a Nuclear-Weapons-Free Zone in Northeast Asia

Although China and France both received strong criticism over their nuclear testing, the distinction was made that China's strategic objective in testing—bringing its nuclear arsenal to the level of U.S. and Russian

14

capabilities—was of particular import. Many in the Study Group thought China should be included in future arms reduction talks. This was a marked shift from the policy position advocated in the Group's initial report, which envisaged START III negotiations limited to the United States and Russia and the inclusion of China in nuclear disarmament talks only after a significant U.S.–Russian build-down had occurred. Others, however, saw Chinese involvement in START III negotiations as a complete non-starter.

There was general consensus that START III discussions should begin as soon possible and need not be contingent upon the U.S. Congress and the Russian Duma ratifying START II. The Study Group expressed great concern that U.S. plans for a ballistic missile defense effort may violate the ABM Treaty and complicate START II ratification by the Duma. Others argued that START III talks should be linked with the CTBT and should at some point draw in not only China but also Great Britain and France. Some posited that START III needed to go beyond the number of warheads and focus on the amount of weapons-grade fissile material held by various countries. The Group was unanimous in its support of further studies defining strategic stability in a multipolar world. Moreover, the Group felt greater study should be devoted to defensive nuclear capabilities, TMD, and the expansion of the ABM Treaty into a multilateral vehicle.

If China's goal is to catch up with U.S. and Russian strategic nuclear capabilities, then the establishment of a nuclear-free zone in Northeast Asia will become an increasingly attractive option for the region. However, on the issue of a nuclear-weapons-free zone (NWFZ), contrasting views were expressed by members of the Study Group. One line of reasoning posited that, if northeast Asia became a NWFZ, a U.S. military presence in Asia, which involves the potential deployment of nuclear forces, would be in jeopardy. Others argued that a NWFZ would strengthen Asia's developing non-proliferation efforts. As the urgent response to North Korea's nuclear aspirations demonstrated, nuclear weapons on the Korean Peninsula—reunified or separated—could not be sanctioned in the future. Japan cannot independently prevent a reoccurrence of nuclear arms development in the Koreas, but the inclusion of the peninsula in a NWFZ would be an effective way to forestall proliferation.

The issue of negative security assurances (i.e., no first use of nuclear weapons) generated significant debate within the Study Group. Such assurances were deemed acceptable by some, but they were considered by many to undermine the overall effectiveness of the U.S. deterrent. In light of the post–Cold War security environment in Asia, it was argued, negative security assurances could jeopardize the U.S.–

Japan and U.S.–Republic of Korea security alliances. The discussion focused on the Korean Peninsula. North Korea sought negative security assurances during the nuclear freeze negotiations. It assumed that a Type A U.S. nuclear umbrella—i.e., the possible first use of nuclear weapons in the event of conventional war—now applies to South Korea, and that its goal is to neutralize this possibility through negative security assurances obtained from the United States. An American member reminded the group that, while a nuclear umbrella over the Korean Peninsula did exist, it had changed in many ways. Even though the United States did not give any negative security assurances to North Korea, the Agreed Framework envisaged such assurances at a later date.

Negative security assurances with respect to North Korea would require the approval of South Korea, and therein lies a trade-off—a Type B nuclear umbrella (i.e., a U.S. pledge to use nuclear weapons only in response to the first use of nuclear weapons by a nuclear power) in exchange for a denuclearized Korean Peninsula (i.e., North Korean cooperation in IAEA inspections adequate to assure that it does not have a nuclear weapons capability).

Global Approach to Non-Proliferation

The Study Group also examined three major sub-topics relating to non-proliferation at the global level: (1) strengthening the NPT; (2) U.S.–Japan cooperation on export controls; and (3) the use of plutonium in the future. The Study Group was unanimous in its support for strengthening the NPT and for pursuing nuclear arms control measures in order to stabilize support for the NPT. It was deemed critically important to implement START II and to begin discussions on START III as a concomitant to non-proliferation efforts. Moreover, the United States, Russia, and others should avoid actions that undermine the START process. For example, many ballistic missile defense (BMD) proposals would clearly jeopardize the ABM Treaty. From the Japanese perspective, the successful implementation of the Agreed Framework with North Korea is essential for the future success of non-proliferation both in and beyond Asia. Above all, the Group agreed, there is a need for a fresh look at nuclear strategy by the United States and Russia and by the United States and Japan. Russian policy appears headed in the wrong direction, the Group felt, since the Russian conventional military force melt-down is being offset by greater emphasis on its nuclear arsenal.

The Study Group concluded that the need for greater debate on nuclear issues is acute in both Japan and the United States. Public indifference has led to a gross misallocation of political resources, exemplified by political protest over French nuclear testing in Japan, while little interest is shown in French sales of arms and technology in the region.

Any new debate should attempt to completely restructure current policy in terms of nuclear strategy around the world. Most troubling to the Group were the many basic questions still unanswered. What is a minimum deterrent posture? How low can such a posture go? Is there a reliable safeguard against the resurgence of a belligerent, albeit less well-armed, Russia? Does a science background help policy makers in shaping nuclear policy? Are democratic procedures compatible with the safe management of nuclear weapons?

The Group was supportive of greater bilateral cooperation in the area of export controls. One obstacle to further cooperation noted is the lack of a shared definition of the requirements of the post-COCOM era.[5] Communist regimes are no longer the primary concern in export control, but where current concern should be centered is not clear. This transition needs to be addressed by the United States and Japan. Questions regarding dual-use technology also need to be reassessed in the post-COCOM environment.

In addition to its discussion of the regional security impact of Japan's plutonium program summarized above, the Group considered the broader issues posed by plutonium-based nuclear programs around the world. Many American members perceived a direct relationship between plutonium use and nuclear proliferation. Japanese members did not share this perspective.

The costs and benefits of using plutonium rather than uranium were a major focus of the discussion. There was agreement that much of the long-term cost calculation of plutonium use depends on the level of regulation or deregulation in a particular country. In any event, a Japanese member explained, Japan's utilization of plutonium is not based on economic or cost factors alone, but also involves environmental factors. Concerned about global warming, coupled with nearby China's heavy and increasing reliance on coal-based power, Japan weighs the economic costs of using plutonium against environmental benefits. It was noted by an American member, however, that any real environmental advantage is slight; Japan's nuclear waste is currently encased in glass and can be stored above ground for only 50 to 100 years. Most American participants did not feel that environmental factors justified the use of plutonium in nuclear power. On the issue of radioactive waste, there was also a clear division between Japanese and American Group members.

Japanese members cited the continued depletion of coal, oil, and uranium, in addition to emphasizing the environmental advantages of plutonium. They pointed to projections showing that an increase in Chinese nuclear power plants will force the country to become a net uranium importer. Moreover, they estimated that, by the year 2013, China would be recycling plutonium. Americans in the Study Group acknowledged that breeder reactors may be required in the future, but argued that their existence today was not justified by market factors. If uranium prices were attractive, they said, there would be an increase in supply, since breeders use both plutonium and uranium. It is misleading to roll out the resource depletion argument against a "once-through" system, since all natural resources are finite. In the context of increasing pressure to make hydrocarbon fuels more available to newly industrializing countries (NICs), the Group agreed that the calculus in determining East Asia's future energy needs will remain a complex matter.

Much of the discussion in this area focused on global issues, on which it was felt cooperation between the United States and Japan would be useful, but not determining. Still, the study brought into sharper relief the differences that exist between the policy communities in the two countries on these critical issues, and it suggests the need for continued discussion to narrow these differences.

Fissile Material Security

The Study Group reaffirmed the importance of fissile missile security. There was regret that the United States, Japan, and Russia have not worked together more effectively on this problem. Members on both sides were concerned that, in the absence of tight political control, Russian fissile material is quite vulnerable to theft and misappropriation. Efforts to improve the situation are moving very slowly. Outside of concerned circles in the United States, this problem receives very little attention. Yet it will remain with us for years and, should there be a major breach of the system, the viability of the NPT will be called into question.

The Study Group saw a strong need to increase collaboration between the United States and Japan with respect to the security of Russian fissile materials. By law, the United States is required to inspect all facilities, domestic and foreign, where U.S. fissile materials are kept. Japan was recently rated excellent by U.S. authorities. In terms of cooperation, the United States and Japan could work jointly to train Russian technicians as well as those of other nations in protecting fissile materials. Moreover, the U.S. side believed, Japan should use its aid funds to advance non-proliferation objectives.

Despite the disturbing reports presented to the Group about Russian fissile-materials protection, the Group noted that there have been no major breaches of security to date and that a mechanism for protecting fissile materials at weapon-grade levels is currently in place. Special concern was expressed about moving materials currently protected by the military to storage facilities under civilian control. Interagency procedures relating to dismantling missiles exist between various Russian ministries, but they are not transparent.

While welcoming recent security improvements, the Group cautioned that the entire Russian apparatus is still vulnerable to the conspiracies of a few. Bulk handling and reprocessing plants are operated according to world standards, yet 30-40 kilograms of material can still go unaccounted for because the accounting system is not in balance.

The Russian nuclear problem is one that has been addressed in many different arenas. Still, given Japan's proximity to Russia and U.S. global concerns, this is an area where much greater joint effort should be expended and where a meaningful three-way dialogue would be valuable.

CONCLUSION

The specific conclusions and recommendations presented in *The United States, Japan, and the Future of Nuclear Weapons* and in the four working group reports in these pages will, we hope, contribute to the discussion of policy options in the two countries. While solutions were not found to some of the more vexing issues addressed, differences were narrowed and in several instances eliminated. As with all such studies, many areas that require further study were identified.

The Co-Chairmen would like to extend their thanks to all those who participated for their patience, thoughtfulness, and dedication to addressing and seeking to resolve some of the most serious issues facing our two nations. In particular, we would like to thank the U.S. Project Director, Selig S. Harrison; the Japanese Project Director, Akio Watanabe; and, above all, the United States–Japan Foundation and the Center for Global Partnership, whose support made this effort possible.

Notes

[1] Lee Howell, CSIS Fellow in Japan Affairs, contributed to this report.

[2] See *The United States, Japan, and The Future of Nuclear Weapons: Report of the U.S.–Japan Study Group on Arms Control and Non-Proliferation After the Cold War* (Washington, D.C.: Carnegie Endowment for International Peace, 1995), p. 13.

[3] Remarks by Secretary of State Warren Christopher to the NPT Review and Extension Conference, April 17, 1995.

[4] See Research Institute for Peace and Security (Tokyo), *Asian Security: 1995-1996* (London: Brassey's, 1995), p. 29.

[5] COCOM (Coordinating Committee on Export Controls)—now defunct—was a Cold War export-control regime sponsored by the United States to block access of the communist states to strategic commodities.

I.

SECURITY AND ARMS CONTROL IN ASIA

WORKING GROUP I

Co-Chairmen
William H. Gleysteen, Jr., and Akio Watanabe

William Clark, Jr.
Kiyofuku Chuma
Selig S. Harrison
Shigeo Hiramatsu
Spurgeon M. Keeny
Hideya Kurata

SECURITY AND ARMS CONTROL IN ASIA

REPORT OF WORKING GROUP I

T
he working group agreed that historical rivalries and tensions remain a powerful factor shaping defense policies in East Asia. China and Japan demonstrate unmistakable wariness toward each other's potential for regional hegemony; similar anxiety about the great powers significantly complicates the defense policies of smaller Asian nations; and virtually all of East Asia would worry if a revived Russia expanded its influence in the region. These strains are more, not less, apparent than during the Cold War. Fortunately, they have been effectively checked by other forces, particularly rapid economic development, growing interdependence, and the substantial U.S. military presence in the region.

The working group was less certain about the extent and reasons why China and Japan appear as potential threats to others. One member questioned whether China in fact poses a threat beyond its traditional borders; others pointed with concern to China's increasing military budgets, force modernization, nuclear testing, expansive definition of borders, and blatant bullying of Taiwan. Combined with China's sheer size and "middle kingdom" attitude, these features of Chinese behavior disturb neighbors—and other nations. Similarly, Japan's commendable post-war behavior has not erased Chinese and Korean memories of Japanese aggression. The steady growth of Japan's defense forces, its plutonium energy program, and its great technical and economic power were recognized as sources of possible concern.

Given these strains, both Japan and the United States should engage China in ways that encourage economic interdependence, regional cooperation (e.g., regarding Korea), dialogue and transparency in military matters, and other kinds of confidence-building measures. In terms of *realpolitik*, Japanese sanctions against Chinese nuclear testing—understandable symbolism for a domestic audience—did not deter China. A combination of verbal protest and pressure toward a comprehensive test ban might have been a better response. Similarly, American and Japanese efforts toward constructive relations with China are a more promising source of security for Taiwan than unyielding criticism of China's heavy-handed behavior. With one possible exception, however, no one suggested the slightest modification of fundamental policy—i.e., insisting that China resolve its differences with Taiwan by peaceful means.

THE AMERICAN PRESENCE

D espite some ambivalence about the U.S. role in the region (i.e., vis-à-vis China, Russia, and North Korea), the American military presence is critically important to East Asia's strategic equilibrium, because it helps balance and buffer regional tensions. The U.S.–Japan alliance is bedrock for this stabilizing function and should be preserved for the foreseeable future. The alliance must nevertheless adjust to changing circumstances, such as the absence of an apparent common threat in the region, the surge in China's power, shifting relationships in Korea, and growing regionalism in East Asia. Prolonged U.S.–Japan confrontations over trade issues may jeopardize this process.

Although members generally favored maintaining the U.S.–Japan Security Treaty in its present form, they urged that operations under the Treaty accommodate significant changes in the security environment, particularly Japan's evolving leadership role, the Korea factor, and the need to respond more effectively to the concerns of China and other "outside" countries. Gradual adjustment within existing institutions should ease negative reactions to change. Reconfiguration of U.S. forces stationed under the Treaty may eventually be desirable, but there is little prospect that these forces could be redistributed to other parts of Asia or that bilateral American security treaties could be replaced by an effective multilateral mechanism.

KOREA

K orea poses both the region's most dangerous flash point and its most obvious target for arms control. The United States and Japan should be firm in supporting South Korea's defense, pressing for a North-South dialogue, and insisting on full South Korean participation in discussion of arrangements to supersede the Armistice Agreement. At the same time, they should be flexible and persistent in negotiations for a nuclear accord and normalization with North Korea, and they should urge South Korea to adopt positive policies consistent with its unquestioned superiority in relation to the North. Rejecting North Korea's transparent effort to subordinate South Korea's status, most members—not all—opposed experimenting with North Korea's desire to initiate separate talks with U.S. military representatives.

The Working Group favored steady pressure to achieve the denuclearization of North and South Korea as well as reduced confrontation at the Demilitarized Zone (DMZ) by means of carefully balanced confidence-building measures. This process is obviously inhibited by current conditions in North Korea. There is a danger that conditions may deteriorate further; yet, it is not too soon to contemplate and explore terms of a peace treaty as well as the North/South force reductions, U.S. force configuration, and security guarantees that would appropriately accompany an era of constructive co-existence or unification of North and South Korea. In this context, the Group was deeply skeptical about reports that North Korea is now prepared indefinitely to accept an American military presence.

THEATER MISSILE DEFENSE

Discussion of theater missile defense (TMD) was inconclusive and controversial. With varying degrees of intensity, American members cautioned about the reliability and costs of TMD as well as the danger of undermining the ABM Treaty. They noted that TMD measures ostensibly taken against a North Korean threat would disturb China and Russia, probably leading both to increase missiles targetable on Japan and South Korea. While acknowledging these dangers, Japanese members noted that North Korea was a real source of concern, that the U.S. nuclear umbrella seemed less reliable to Japanese in today's circumstances, and that there was much irony in nuclear and missile-armed China's complaints about TMD or Japan's nuclear energy program. The Group agreed only on the need to proceed cautiously.

ASIAN SECURITY: THE FOCUS ON CHINA

WILLIAM H. GLEYSTEEN, JR.

IMPORTANCE OF STRATEGIC EQUILIBRIUM

In a European context, "arms control" usually conjures up images of confidence-building measures, mechanisms for dialogue and transparency of military expenditures, inspection regimes, notification procedures, demilitarized or nuclear-free zones, mutual restraint, and multilateral security arrangements. In East Asia, progress in these directions has been minimal, and successful arms control will depend heavily on a very traditional factor: the degree of stability that can be maintained in the regional balance of power.

Despite important shifts over the past few decades in the way power is distributed and aligned among nations in East Asia, longstanding rivalries and anxieties within the region not only persist but have become more apparent since the end of the Cold War. China and Japan frequently reveal their wariness of each other's potential for regional hegemony; Koreans (both South and North) harbor deep suspicions of Japan, while Japanese are uncomfortable with many aspects of Korea (particularly a unified Korea); Southeast Asians in varying degrees acknowledge their concern not to be overpowered by either Japan or China; and, in a more latent sense, both Chinese and Japanese worry that a revived Russia will eventually resume efforts to expand its influence in the region. China is a party—either directly or indirectly—in all these concerns. The United States is seen as a relatively benign influence.

These powerful, generally subterranean tensions are one of the fundamental factors shaping defense policies (e.g., the buildup of Southeast Asian air forces or the improvement of Chinese blue-water naval capabilities), and, even in fairly normal conditions, they intensify the danger of military confrontation in areas such as the Korea Peninsula or the Taiwan Straits. In circumstances of domestic upheaval or leadership competition for a nationalist mantle, the tensions and emotions underlying them could easily dominate national decisions in profoundly dangerous ways.

Keeping these tensions in check is arguably the highest priority for arms control efforts in a region where historical and geopolitical facts of life still conspire against schemes requiring complex international cooperation. Fortunately, the danger has been effectively muffled in recent years by a variety of factors, particularly rapid economic development and reform policies, growing interdependence within the region, and the maintenance of a fairly steady American presence—both military and economic—in the Western Pacific.

Although there is a fair prospect that this muffling process can continue, success will depend on a number of uncontrollable variables, such as the state of the world economy, and a degree of international understanding and skill that sometimes seems beyond the capacity of key governments:

- To an extraordinary degree, East Asian stability depends on a pattern of improving economic and social status shared by most countries and key groups within countries. Without this sense of improvement and general fairness, the problems of corruption control, income distribution, and other administrative challenges, as well as the turmoil of leadership transition, could overwhelm China and several other countries.

- Nationalism, which in past years has been channeled mostly into support of economic and social development, could in less propitious circumstances be diverted into the international arena— deliberately, for example, by leaders contending with each other for popularity in China and Taiwan, or less wittingly by leaders in the United States who fail to appreciate the attitudinal sea-change of national pride that has accompanied Asia's rapid economic advance.

- Without the discipline imposed by the Cold War, domestic events and vested interests now play a much larger role than in the past, increasing the element of unpredictability and sometimes jeopardizing international stability and prosperity.

- Some Asians, particularly the Chinese, remain ambivalent about the stabilizing role played by the American military presence in East Asia, while many Americans question the need for the United States to undertake this role in the absence of a clear and present danger.

Given these risks, it is quite disturbing that recent U.S. policy toward China and Japan has tended to shortchange the objective of Asian regional stability in favor of factors creating strain. This criticism does not, of course, negate the massive contribution the United States has made to East Asia's current strategic equilibrium. Nor can the United States be held responsible for unpredictable contingencies beyond its control; for new complexities of foreign relations in post–Cold War conditions; or for the fact that China is an exceptionally difficult international partner whose conduct sometimes necessitates very firm opposition and causes inescapable friction.

Nevertheless, measured by the standards of coherence and priority of interests, American policy toward China has been seriously flawed. Granting that some quiet successes have been achieved (e.g., cooperation regarding North Korean nuclear proliferation) and some basic errors corrected (e.g., separating human rights from most-favored-nation (MFN) and trade matters), the Clinton Administration has wobbled on basic issues, given excessive emphasis to human rights, and allowed minority opinions to roll through the Congress. To try to stop this damaging kind of spin, the United States must once again review its national priorities, openly debate them if necessary, and then the President himself, as well as his administration, must educate the Congress and the public to the rationale for these priorities and the trade-offs involved.

Enjoying a wider consensus on China and lacking the missionary zeal of America, Japan has been nearer the mark in what is needed for regional stability and arms control considerations. Conscious of China's manifest anxiety about the re-emergence of a strong neighbor, Japan has been remarkably steady in its efforts to engage China economically and to foster friendly ties. And it has been reasonably successful (excepting perhaps its belated and clumsy efforts to deal with the legacy of the war against China and the way it introduced China and the rest of the world to its plutonium energy program). This sensible political stance toward China has, of course, been economically beneficial.

STRAIN POINTS

In addition to coherence about the fundamentals of regional stability, arms control prospects will critically depend on skilled management of dangerous strain points.

North Korean Nuclear Proliferation

Apart from raising a serious general threat to security, successful nuclear proliferation by North Korea would reopen the question of South Korea's and Japan's future nuclear posture. Therefore South Korea, Japan, and the United States should persist with the Korean Energy Development Organization (KEDO) project, even if progress often resembles guerrilla warfare. As long as North Korea does not actually resume reprocessing, delays in the project or its ultimate failure will be more costly to North Korea than to other KEDO members. Were reprocessing to resume, movement toward sanctions would be irresistible even in the face of Chinese opposition, and some focus on the defensive capabilities of forces in South Korea would help to undergird diplomacy. But since neither the North Korean nor the American people seem willing to go to war over the issue, discussion of military options should be firmly muted, at least in official circles. China has a vital interest in trying to prevent a crisis in North Korea, and even though it may play its role with frustrating caution, it should be given enough leeway to do so.

Korean Unification or "Constructive Co-Existence"

Collapse of the North Korean regime could create a dangerous situation, conceivably leading to Chinese intervention, unless maximum restraint were exercised by South Korea and its allies. On the other hand, a "soft landing" would pose a welcome challenge to constructive arms control if it involved stabilization of North Korea and some form of constructive co-existence with South Korea leading to ultimate unification. At a minimum, there would be the opportunity for a staged and monitored reduction of massive military forces deployed north and south of the demilitarized zone. Quite possibly there would be the opportunity, if not necessity, to re-configure or deploy U.S. forces as well as to seek some sort of multilateral agreement on Korea.

Taiwan

Over the last two years, an unfortunate combination of domestic and international events in Taiwan, the United States, and China has led to a crisis in which Taiwan has pushed its luck near the limit, China has worried many neighbors by its crude threats, and the United States has been damaged by a costly wobble of judgment. Second thoughts in Taipei, Beijing, and Washington, combined with Taiwan's geographic protection from easy military attack, will probably allow repairs to relationships and a gradual return toward the status quo ante. This will, however, necessitate a major effort to restrain Taiwan's exuberance in pursuing international status and an equally difficult American effort to convince China that the United States will not compromise its "one China" commitment. Success may require two apparently contradictory moves: (1) a decision to actually implement the U.S. Administration's lip service to the goal of "engagement" with China; and (2) a low-key, deliberately ambiguous message to Taipei and Beijing about the United States' potential military posture in a heightened crisis. Taipei needs to be reminded that it does not have an automatic guarantee of American military support, while Beijing needs to be reminded that peaceful resolution of the Taiwan problem was a fundamental premise of U.S. normalization of relations with the People's Republic of China (PRC).

The Spratly Islands

Although a real solution to conflicting claims in the Spratly Islands may be extremely difficult, if not impossible, in today's conditions the problem should, nevertheless, be manageable without a major crisis. It is a prime candidate for multilateral treatment in an arms control context with Southeast Asian nations playing a major role. Japan and the United States should limit themselves to firm support for a peaceful solution and statements that international transit through the area is a vital interest.

CONCLUSION

The East Asian region is not ripe for elaborate arms control schemes, and the greatest contribution the United States and Japan can make is to ensure stability of the regional equilibrium and skillful management of periodic crises. Some recent American behavior has violated these fundamentals, either out of ignorance or because of domestic pressures. There is reason to hope that future policy will be governed by a more coherent set of priorities.

ASIAN SECURITY: THE FOCUS ON CHINA

SHIGEO HIRAMATSU

RECORD OF NUCLEAR WEAPONS DEVELOPMENT IN CHINA

China has repeated nuclear tests almost every year since its first test in October 1964. It succeeded in launching an intercontinental ballistic missile (ICBM) in May 1980 and a submarine-launched ballistic missile (SLBM) in October 1982 in tests that were part of its effort to develop nuclear weapons. These successes marked the end of China's first generation of nuclear weapons development; it had acquired a second-strike capability or the "minimum nuclear deterrent," since at least part of its nuclear arsenal could be expected to survive an initial attack. To gain the capability of retaliating more quickly, flexibly, and reliably, and to achieve high survivability, China faced the tasks of reducing the size and weight of its nuclear warheads, implementing solid-fuel rocket propulsion, developing missiles that could be launched from mobile launchers as well as nuclear submarines and ballistic missiles for that platform, and developing tactical nuclear weapons.

The new development efforts that began in the mid-1980s are expected to produce—throughout the latter half of the 1990s into the beginning of the next century—at least three types of second-generation nuclear weapons. These are: the Dong Feng 41, with a range of 12,000 km, capable of delivering a warhead to the eastern United States; the Dong Feng 31, with a range of 8,000 km, capable of striking the western United States if launched from the ground and all of the United States if launched from a submarine; and the Dong Feng 25, with a range of 1,700 km, capable of carrying a two-ton conventional warhead.

On May 15, 1995, four days after a majority of the signatory countries had agreed on an unlimited extension of the Nuclear Non-Proliferation Treaty (NPT), China conducted a nuclear test in defiance of world opinion. On the same day, China announced the closure of an entire nuclear weapons research and production base in Qing Hai, in compliance with a decision made in 1987. The base was the first of its kind to be constructed in China; its closure implied that production of first-generation nuclear warheads had ceased and that production of second-generation warheads is under way. On May 29, two weeks after the announcement, China performed a test launch of the new Dong Feng 31 ICBM, which can be launched from a mobile platform.

In July 1995, China fired six missiles into the sea in a launch test conducted north of Taiwan. Four were presumed to be the M-9 short-range ballistic missiles and the remaining two, Dong Feng 21 intermediate-range ballistic missiles.

Moreover, on the day the ICBM test launch took place, Beijing issued a statement that tens of thousands of soldiers in the Second Artillery, China's strategic rocket force, had after over ten years of arduous labor completed construction of a large citadel. Although the purpose of this new citadel is unclear, it is presumably a base for launching ballistic missiles, and its location is not known.

Since China has not completed its development of nuclear weapons, it undoubtedly intends to perform future nuclear and missile tests. U.S. Secretary of Defense William Perry visited China in October 1994 and said that Beijing informed him that there would be five nuclear tests over the next two years. On that occasion, Mr. Perry took the position that nuclear tests should be halted in advance of the anticipated conclusion of the Comprehensive Test Ban Treaty (CTBT) in 1996. He proposed that the United States provide China with simulation technology that would enable it to obtain results comparable to those of nuclear tests. According to Mr. Perry, China showed interest in obtaining this technology. Mr. Perry was accompanied on his visit by an official of the Department of State's Arms Control and Disarmament Agency in charge of U.S. efforts to prevent the proliferation of weapons of mass destruction. On October 4, immediately before the talks were to begin, the United States and China reached an understanding on the Missile Technology Control Regime (MTCR).

PERSISTENT DOUBTS ABOUT CHINESE TRANSFERS OF NUCLEAR WEAPONS TECHNOLOGIES

China began its missile exports in the 1980s—with an immense sale of surface-to-surface Silkworm anti-ship missiles to Iran during the Iran-Iraq War. Then, in 1988, while the war was continuing, it sold surface-to-surface intermediate-range missiles with a range of 3,500 km to Saudi Arabia. A little later in the same year, rumors grew that China had sold M-9 short-range ballistic missiles to Syria.

In or around 1992, just after the Gulf War, it was rumored that China had sold M-11 short-range ballistic missiles to Pakistan. The M-9 and M-11 are China's most modern ballistic missiles; they can be armed with small nuclear warheads and launched from mobile launchers. In August 1993, disregarding denials by both China and Pakistan, the United States concluded that China had exported M-11 technology to Pakistan in violation of the understanding on the MTCR and invoked economic sanctions prohibiting the export of high-technology equipment and other products to China. Though not a party to the MTCR agreement, China had promised in 1991 to observe the guidelines in the agreement barring the export of missiles able to carry a 500-kg payload over a range of 300 km (186 mi). In response to the U.S. sanctions, China continued to deny that it had exported M-11 technology to Pakistan. It protested that the MTCR guidelines had been tightened without consulting Beijing and that China would therefore reconsider its policy of complying with the MTCR. On October 4, 1994, the United States lifted economic sanctions in exchange for a Chinese pledge reaffirming its agreement to adhere to the MTCR. Besides the rumors suggesting that China was supplying missiles to Pakistan, doubts were also raised as to the nature of a nuclear-power station constructed by China in Iran. In mid-June 1995, the U.S. Central Intelligence Agency submitted a report to President Clinton that claimed China was exporting ballistic missile technology to Iran. If U.S. economic sanctions are reimposed against China as a consequence, in retaliation for alleged MTCR violations, this would inflict serious damage to China–U.S. trade, which amounted to $27 billion in 1993.

The Clinton Administration, intent on maintaining American access to Chinese markets, has continued since 1995 to seek to persuade Beijing to observe the MTCR guidelines, with the incentive that the United States would be willing to overlook previous violations. The United States once took the same tack in opposing a Soviet attempt to sell rocket engines to India; in that case, American pressure led to the cancellation of the deal. According to an agreement reached on April 17, 1995, in talks between the Chinese Minister of Foreign Affairs Qian Qi Chen and U.S. Secretary of State Warren Christopher in New York, China promised the United States that it would observe the understanding on the MTCR.

RESUMPTION OF MILITARY EXCHANGES AND INTERRUPTION OF ARMS CONTROL AND DISARMAMENT NEGOTIATIONS

The visit of U.S. Assistant Secretary of Defense (for Regional Security) Charles Freeman to China in October-November 1993 marked the resumption of China–U.S. military talks and exchanges which had been suspended since the Tiananmen Square incident of June 1989.

Assistant Secretary Freeman stated in China that, with great changes occurring in the world since 1989, including the collapse of the Soviet Union, the China–U.S. military relationship of the 1980s, which had been formed solely in pursuit of strategic cooperation to put pressure on Moscow, was now obsolete. He thus suggested that the new military relationship between the two countries was essentially different from the earlier one. For the United States, China was no longer a "threat," but an important "potential partner" with whom to negotiate on arms control and disarmament and consult on Asian security in the process of developing U.S. global strategies and defense policies.

China's military strength, while still small compared with that of the more developed countries, is undergoing vigorous modernization. The growth of its nuclear capacity is particularly striking. Sustained economic growth may raise China to the status of a military giant in Asia by the end of this century or the beginning of the next.

The progress of China-Russia military cooperation, which includes the transfer of weapons and military technologies, lies behind this military development. It is quite natural that the Clinton Administration is striving to get Beijing to negotiate on arms control and disarmament, having come to realize that a China–U.S. military dialogue and exchange is indispensable—especially after observing that China's growing military power is becoming a threat to nearby Asian nations and that China has been disseminating nuclear weapons and related technologies to other Third World countries.

The Clinton Administration also has a pressing need to forge political ties with the Chinese military, which has been playing a major role in policy formation and will be a key factor in "post-Deng" Chinese politics. The U.S. Administration is seriously concerned, in this context, about the possibility of nuclear weapons proliferation amidst the political confusion and instability likely to arise in post-Deng China.

In an effort to attain such vital ends, the Clinton Administration promoted military exchanges with China by dispatching Secretary of Defense William Perry to China in October 1994. The United States was expected to have the Chinese Minister of National Defense Chi Haotian visit in June 1995 to promote the military exchange, and to declare China's willingness to enter into arms control and disarmament negotiations with the United States and hold a joint meeting of experts on the subject.

But the visit of Taiwanese President Lee Teng-hui to the United States in June 1995—a visit that was significant in demonstrating to the world the closeness of the Taiwan–U.S. relationship and Taiwan's economic success and democratization—had serious consequences. The Chinese refused to participate in arms control and disarmament negotiations with the United States, and Beijing postponed not only the scheduled June visit of its Minister of National Defense to the United States but also the meeting of experts on MTCR and nuclear cooperation. Also postponed were the visits to China by the Chief of the U.S. Arms Control and Disarmament Agency and the State Department's Assistant Secretary for Political and Military Affairs, which had been planned for June and July 1995, respectively.

Explaining that allowing President Lee of Taiwan to visit the United States did not contradict Washington's "single China policy" and that military exchanges between the United States and China benefit both parties, the United States appealed to Beijing to resume the exchanges. But Beijing has rebuffed this appeal and does not conceal its mistrust of the Clinton Administration.

Even though China has repeatedly held nuclear and missile tests and concern has mounted about its sale of nuclear weapons and related technologies to Third World countries, Washington has made strenuous efforts to engage China in arms-control talks. The Chinese reaction to President Lee's visit was a great setback to the United States. China will perhaps continue its nuclear tests and weapons sales to Third World countries. But one cannot simply assume that the U.S.–China arms control and disarmament negotiations might have progressed well if President Lee had not visited the United States. The task of organizing negotiations with China is, however, back to where it started.

It is unlikely that either the United States or China will abandon the "economy first" principle and that U.S.–China relations will change drastically for the worse, even though there may be incessant friction between the two countries. The questions of how the United States can find a way to resume negotiations on the important problem of arms control and disarmament and how China will respond continue to be matters of great concern.

THE KOREAN PENINSULA: CURRENT PROBLEMS, FUTURE PROSPECTS

SELIG S. HARRISON

Despite dire predictions that North Korea would collapse after the death of President Kim Il Sung and that the U.S.–North Korea nuclear-freeze agreement would unravel, it is increasingly likely that the Pyongyang regime will remain stable in the years ahead and that fears of a North Korean nuclear program will gradually recede. Yet dangerous North-South military tensions persist, posing continuing danger of another conventional war on the Korean Peninsula unless serious arms control measures are adopted.

It is now forty-two years since the Armistice Agreement was signed on July 27, 1953. With the Cold War over and Washington committed to exchanging liaison offices with Pyongyang, the time has clearly come to replace the Armistice Agreement with more stable arrangements designed to ensure peace in the Korean Peninsula.

It is not enough for Washington and Seoul to say that peace in Korea is a matter strictly between North and South and that peace can be stabilized by simply honoring the North-South agreements concluded in December 1991. While the 1991 accords should be carried out, they should be accompanied by broader arrangements involving the United States. The path to peace and reunification does not lie exclusively in a bilateral U.S.–North Korean peace treaty or bilateral North-South agreements, but in a trilateral pattern of negotiations in which the United States joins in shaping and implementing what the North has variously called a "new peace mechanism," "new peace system," and "new peace arrangements."

THE OBSOLETE ARMISTICE

As a North Korean Foreign Ministry statement on May 12, 1995, observed, "the armistice system defines the bilateral relations of the DPRK [Democratic People's Republic of Korea] and the United States as those of hostile parties" and is thus incompatible with the normalization of relations envisaged in the October 1994 nuclear freeze agreement. Given the U.S. force presence in the South, the U.S. mutual security treaty with Seoul, and U.S. operational control over South Korean forces in the event of a war, Pyongyang correctly points out that it would be unrealistic to exclude the United States from "new peace arrangements."

Legally, the United States and North Korea are indeed enemies. The 1953 Armistice has never been replaced by a peace treaty, and the U.N. Command established to fight the Korean War is still the legal basis for the American presence. Significantly, however, the North no longer demands a bilateral peace treaty with the United States excluding the South. North Korean officials now say that a formal peace treaty can wait. They point to the fact that Japan does not have peace treaties with Russia or China. But they do say that replacing the Armistice with what they call a "new peace mechanism" is a precondition for diplomatic relations.

During a visit to Pyongyang from September 19-26, 1995, I spent four hours with General Ri Chan Bok, the representative of the Korean People's Army at Panmunjon. He made a new proposal for a two-track peacekeeping system to replace the Armistice machinery—a proposal that would basically alter the role of the United States in the Korean Peninsula. First, the U.S. and North Korean armed forces would set up something that might be called a Mutual Security Commission, consisting of representatives of the U.S. and North Korean armed forces and not the two governments. Then, once the U.S.–North Korean Commission is agreed upon, the North Korea–South Korea Joint Military Commission would go into operation. The North-South Commission was negotiated in 1992 but never went into effect.

The purpose of both commissions would be to keep the peace, but the inclusion of a strictly U.S.–North Korean body as a part of this would imply a basic change in the U.S. role. At present the United States is in Korea to defend the South against possible North Korean aggression. But the proposed new setup would broaden the U.S. role. The United States would become a stabilizer and balancer for the peninsula as a whole, helping to prevent any threat to the peace—whether from the South against the North or the North against the South. Those are exactly the words used by First Deputy Foreign Minister Kang Sok Ju: "The Armistice was concluded between two hostile parties. By contrast, the United States and the DPRK will conclude the new peace mechanism to guarantee the security of the peninsula as a whole. The new mechanism will help to prevent any threat to the peace, whether from the South against the North or the North against the South."

General Ri Chan Bok emphasized that the North would not object to the presence of U.S. forces once the "new peace mechanism" is established. "The Americans," he said, "think that if they join in establishing the new peace mechanism, we will raise the question of withdrawing troops from the Korean Peninsula. But it's clear from the Asian strategy of the United States that the U.S. army will not pull out tomorrow. It will take a long time. Accordingly, we will set up a new peace mechanism on the basis of a mutual understanding that U.S. forces will continue to be stationed in Korea indefinitely."

Off the record, one of the key officials I met said "Korea is surrounded by big powers—Russia, China, and Japan. We must think of the impact of the withdrawal of U.S. troops on the balance of power in the region." Another said that "If U.S. troops pull out of Korea, Japan will rearm immediately." These officials did not want to be quoted by name but clearly wanted to send a very strong signal.

THE NEED FOR ARMS CONTROL

I responded to the North Korean proposals with some specific proposals of my own concerning how the Armistice could be replaced. My message was that I did not think the United States would terminate the U.N. Command as the basis for the American presence unless tensions at the thirty-eighth parallel were actually reduced. I proposed a mutual North Korea–South Korea–U.S. pullback of offensive forces or, at the very least, significant reductions in offensive forces. I also emphasized that the North-South Military Commission should go into effect simultaneously with the proposed U.S.–North Korean Commission and should be closely coordinated with it—perhaps within one combined overall structure.

South Korea argues that the North should talk to the South first about the replacement of the Armistice in order to adopt a common Korean position on the role that the United States and perhaps China should play in any "new peace mechanism." Washington, deferring to the South, has rejected the North's overtures for meetings at the level of generals to discuss a new approach to Korean peacekeeping. In my view, this is a mistake. Forty-two years after the Korean War, it is time for the United States to put forward the terms and conditions that would make it possible to replace the Armistice and terminate the U.N. Command.

The United States should recast its role in Korea to suit the new realities of the post–Cold War period. The U.S. alliance with the South made geopolitical sense in 1953 because the North was allied with the Soviet Union and China. But now Russia and China have closer relations with South Korea than with the North. The United States finds itself involved on one side of a civil war in which both sides want to be its friends.

For the foreseeable future, the United States should keep its ground forces in the South, pending substantial progress in North-South arms control measures, including a mutual pullback of offensive forces from an agreed zone on both sides of the thirty-eighth parallel. However, while honoring its military obligations to Seoul under the Mutual Security Treaty, the United States should adopt a more flexible diplomatic and political posture and should not be hostage to the South in pursuing friendship with the North. The American objective should be to play the role of stabilizer and balancer envisioned in General Ri's proposal, promoting a reduction of tensions and a loose confederation based on the co-existence of differing systems. Such a role would facilitate a peaceful unification process and the emergence of a neutral Korean buffer state that will help to forestall major power conflict in Northeast Asia.

THE KOREAN PENINSULA: CURRENT PROBLEMS, FUTURE PROSPECTS

HIDEYA KURATA

COMPREHENSIVENESS OF THE AGREED FRAMEWORK

The Agreed Framework between the United States and the Democratic People's Republic of Korea (DPRK), signed on October 21, 1994, is in essence a "deal" between the United States and North Korea. North Korea is to freeze its nuclear activities and ultimately dismantle its graphite-moderated reactors (Article I-3), and the United States is to upgrade bilateral relations to the Ambassadorial level on a gradual basis (Article II-1, 2, 3).[1] The Agreed Framework is composed of four "baskets," and factors other than U.S.–North Korean relations are involved in the deal.

Implementation of the Agreed Framework has three aspects: North Korea's limited external openness, the North-South Korean dialogue, and U.S.–North Korean bilateral relations. Providing light-water reactors (LWRs) to North Korea in exchange for its agreement to a nuclear freeze and dismantling of its graphite-moderated reactors is tied, even if only indirectly, to its limited external openness. It is essential that North Korea permit technicians from the United States and the Republic of Korea (ROK) to operate in North Korea. North Korean participation in the North-South dialogue as well as American assurances to North Korea on the threat or use of U.S. nuclear weapons are stipulated in Article III of the Agreed Framework.

We need to re-examine first the disposition of 8,000 spent-fuel rods extracted from North Korea's 5 MW "experimental reactor," without monitoring by the International Atomic Energy Agency (IAEA) inspectors, which was the focal issue in the case for punitive sanctions in early 1994 prior to the Agreed Framework.

The Agreed Framework stipulates that "as soon as possible after the date of this document U.S. and DPRK experts will hold two sets of expert talks." On the one hand, they were to discuss "the issues related to alternative energy and the replacement of the graphite-moderated reactor program with the LWR project," and on the other, the "specific arrangements for spent fuel storage and ultimate disposition." The two sets of talks were supposed to proceed simultaneously (Article I-4). The Agreed Framework also stipulated, without setting a final date, that "the

U.S. and DPRK will cooperate in finding a method to store safely the spent fuel from the 5 MW(e) experimental reactor during the construction of the LWR project, and to dispose of the fuel in a safe manner that does not involve reprocessing in the DPRK" (Article I-3). The provision of the LWRs was mentioned for the first time in the Press Statement after U.S.–DPRK negotiations in Geneva in July 1993. A clause was added to the effect that such a provision would serve "as part of a final resolution of the nuclear issue."[2] It can be assumed that provision of the LWRs, intended to be the "result" of an overall resolution of the nuclear issue, in fact became a "condition" for North Korea's nuclear freeze. Yet, there is little correlation in time between provision of the LWRs and the nuclear freeze. The Agreed Framework merely states in a vague manner that final resolution of the problems related to the experimental reactor will occur "during construction of the LWR."

Problems of this kind are encountered in other areas as well. The Agreed Framework touches on the North-South dialogue, but it neither specifies at what stage in the process of normalization of U.S.–North Korean relations, nor in what form, the North-South dialogue would begin. Moreover, North Korea does not regard the Agreed Framework as an accord limited to the nuclear problem. In fact, since the autumn of 1993, North Korea has consistently pushed for the conclusion of the "New Peace Arrangement," a peace pact with the United States as a logical companion to the normalization of diplomatic relations envisaged in the Agreed Framework. The proposal was first made during the nuclear controversy, and its focus on U.S.–DPRK relations, as distinct from North-South relations, conflicts with the 1991 "Agreement on Reconciliation and Nonaggression, and Exchange and Cooperation between the North and South" (the Basic Accord). Viewing the Agreed Framework as a document to achieve improvement in its bilateral relations with the United States, North Korea has been pushing for the New Peace Arrangement even more actively.[3]

KUALA LUMPUR AGREEMENT: LWRS AND THE "NEW PEACE ARRANGEMENT"

It was quite natural that diplomatically isolated South Korea should attempt to link the provision of LWRs with resumption of the North-South dialogue. The United States seemed to have had provision of the South Korea Standard LWRs in mind at an early stage. It is well-known that South Korea had introduced the U.S. ABB–Combustion Engineering system with a generating capacity of 1,300 MW in 1984, and succeeded in reducing its capacity to 1,000 MW for use at Yonggwang 3 and 4 units. A further improved model, the Ulchin 3, installed at Ulchin in North Kyongsang Province in South Korea in April 1995 (commercial operation scheduled in 1998) has a 950 MW capacity. "The LWR project with a total generating capacity of approximately 2,000 MW(e)," mentioned in the Agreed Framework (Article I-1), was likely designed to utilize two South Korea Standard LWRs. As a matter of course then, the Agreement on Establishment of the Korean Peninsula Energy Development Organization (KEDO) stipulated for "two reactors of the Korean Standard nuclear plant model with a capacity of approximately 1,000 MW(e) each." (Article II), omitting the word "South" in describing the Standard model as a concession to North Korea.[4]

North Korea's reaction to the KEDO Agreement was harsher than expected. Since the term "Korea Standard LWRs" implies not only reactors but "designs, turbine-generators and all other facilities and procedures,"[5] it was inevitable that South Korean technicians would have to accompany the LWRs to North Korea, prompting North Korea to label the plan a Trojan Horse.

Two problems should be discussed in this context. Both are inseparably related to the structure of the Agreed Framework. The first arises from a stipulation in the Agreed Framework that allows simultaneous progress of talks over the provision of LWRs and over issues related to the experimental reactors. Although the United States and North Korea have discussed the safe storage of spent-fuel rods and the provision of LWRs since January 1995, they have not reached agreement on the final disposition of the spent-fuel rods. This enabled North Korea to threaten to recharge the fuel rods in the experimental reactor to demonstrate its opposition to the supply of South Korea Standard LWRs.

The second problem relates to North Korea's proposal for a "New Peace Arrangement," inasmuch as North Korea does not regard the Agreed Framework as covering only the nuclear problem. On April 19, 1995, linking the New Peace Arrangement to the nuclear problem, a North Korean Foreign Ministry spokesman asserted, "as stated in the Agreed Framework, establishing a 'New Peace Arrangement' and having the United States withdraw its forces from South Korea are the fundamental and most pressing issues in guaranteeing the peace and security of the Korean Peninsula. . . . The implementation of the 'Agreed Framework,' beginning with the provision of the LWRs, will be decisively influenced by the resolution of this problem."[6]

The Kuala Lumpur Agreement of mid-1995 stipulates: "the LWR project will consist of two pressurized light-water reactors with two coolant loops and a generating capacity of approximately 1,000 MW each. The reactor model, selected by KEDO, will be the advanced version of U.S.–origin design and technology currently under construction"

(Article II),[7] implying that the LWRs to be provided should be South Korea Standard Reactors. The Kuala Lumpur Agreement itself is an extension of the Agreed Framework and the Agreement on KEDO, but it states that "the cost of this site preparation of the LWR will be included in the scope of the supply for the project," without referring to South Korea Standard Reactors, which amounted to a big gain for North Korea.

It is hard to imagine that North Korea would willingly accept South Korea Standard LWRs without a fight. In fact, North Korea continues to criticize South Korea Standard LWRs,[8] and disputes on the scope of supply will arise until the contract is concluded. The North Korean negotiator in Kuala Lumpur, Mr. Kim Kye-guan, insisted on the need for the New Peace Arrangement right before the negotiations, but he did not do so during the negotiations. North Korea had to make haste in concluding the LWR supply contract, but this does not necessarily mean that North Korea has dropped its insistence on the New Peace Arrangement. On the contrary, North Korea has increasingly been making proposals for it even after the Kuala Lumpur Agreement was concluded.[9]

COMPENSATION MEASURES FOR "REGIME SECURITY"

Although the Kuala Lumpur Agreement was limited to technological matters, North Korea's posture of viewing U.S.–DPRK relations comprehensively has remained unchanged. It seems that North Korea's need to ease tensions with the United States has strengthened its desire to ensure "Regime Security."

North Korea's major goal in its relations with the United States continues to be to establish the New Peace Arrangement. There is no sign that the United States and South Korea are willing to accept North Korea's position. After the settlement of the nuclear problem, South Korea, which was isolated for more than two years during the course of the U.S.–DPRK talks, is uncompromising in its desire to create a peace regime between North Korea and itself. South Korean President Kim Young Sam in his speech on the anniversary of the national liberation day said "the most urgent problem is to establish a lasting peace regime on the Korean Peninsula," and "the problem of building a peace regime has to be discussed and solved first by North and South Korea."[10] The United States has no reason to accept the New Peace Arrangement, since it has succeeded so far in reaching the Agreed Framework and the Kuala Lumpur Agreement without accepting North Korea's position. For the United States, the next important task is to get North Korea to participate is the North-South dialogue.

It appears that North Korea may show flexibility on reaching the New Peace Arrangement, even though it continues to insist on the need for it. In this context, remarks by high North Korean officials on the peace regime in Korea to Selig Harrison, Senior Research Fellow at the Carnegie Endowment for International Peace, during his September 1995 visit to North Korea are noteworthy. Dividing the New Peace Arrangement into a two-step process, they insisted on organizing a mutual security consultative committee between themselves and the United States as a first step, and expressed readiness to begin operation of the North-South Joint Military Commission envisaged in the Basic Accord after preparations for the U.S.–DPRK committee. Moreover, they reportedly admitted that concluding the peace pact between themselves and the United States is unrealistic.[11]

Attention should be paid to North Korea's positive remarks on putting the North-South Joint Military Commission into operation. But as stated in the Basic Accord, the issue of building a peace regime is to be discussed by the North-South Joint Reconciliation Commission and not by the North-South Joint Military Commission. The fact that the North Koreans did not refer to the former Commission indicates that they do not see South Korea as a party to building a peace regime on the Korean Peninsula.

It goes without saying that the Republic of Korea will not deny the significance of putting the North-South Joint Military Commission into operation, because South Korea considers implementation of confidence-building measures, which is the task of the North-South Joint Military Commission, to be a precondition for establishing a peace regime.[12] Having no choice but to accept the South Korea Standard LWRs, North Korea will inevitably feel a heightened sense of crisis about Regime Security. The new proposals outlined to Selig Harrison should be underscored in this context. The United States, recognizing that resumption of the North-South dialogue is an important item of the Agreed Framework, should not send any premature signals to North Korea on a peace regime until the North-South Joint Reconciliation Commission is in operation.

Notes

[1] Quotations from the Agreed Framework are from "The Agreed Framework between the United States and the Democratic People's Republic of Korea, Geneva, October 21, 1994," *IFANS Review: U.S.–North Korea Nuclear Accord and Inter-Korean Relations*, Vol. 2, No. 8 (December 1994), pp. 27-30. For the diplomatic significance of the Agreed Framework, see Hideya Kurata, "The Triple-layered Structure and Its Disturbance of the Multilateral Arrangements on the Korean Problem" in Tatsumi Okabe, ed., *The Asia-Pacific Region in the Post Cold War Era*, Tokyo: JIIA, 1995, pp. 256-95 (in Japanese).

[2] "Press Statement (Text Agreed by the USA and the DPRK Delegations), Geneva, July 19, 1993," *IFANS Review: North Korea's Nuclear Issue*, Vol. 1, No. 3, December 1993, p. 31.

[3] See Hideya Kurata, "The International Context of North Korea's Proposal for a 'New Peace Arrangement': Issues after the U.S.-DPRK Nuclear Accord," *The Korean Journal of Defense Analysis*, Vol. VII, No. 1, Summer 1995, pp. 251-73.

[4] *White Paper on Atomic Safety* (1994), Seoul: Science and Technology Agency, 1994, pp. 77-78 (in Korean).

[5] "The Agreement on the Establishment of the Korean Peninsula Energy Development Organization (KEDO), Signed by the U.S. and Its Allies, for Supporting ROK-Model Reactors to North Korea, United Nations, New York, March 8, 1995," *Korea and World Affairs*, Vol. XIX, No. 1, Spring 1995, pp. 157-61.

[6] *Rodong Shinmun*, April 19, 1995 (in Korean).

[7] Quotations from the English text of the KL Agreement are taken from "Joint U.S.–North Korean Press Statement on the Provision of Light-Water Reactors (LWRs), Authorizing KEDO to Conclude the Reactor Supply Accord, Kuala Lumpur, Malaysia, June 12, 1995, *Korea and World Affairs*, Vol. XIX, No. 2, Summer 1995, pp. 257-58.

[8] See, for example, *Rodong Shinmun*, June 16, 1995.

[9] See editorial in *Rodong Shinmun*, June 25, 1995 (in Korea), and the memorandum released by North Korea's Foreign Ministry in *Rodong Shinmun*, June 30, 1995 (in Korean). Kim Kye-guan, the North Korean negotiator made the following remark on the provision of LWRs during the talks in Kuala Lumpur: "this is related to the unresolved hostilities between the DPRK and the U.S. and, therefore, a peace pact must be concluded between the DPRK and the U.S." See, *Seoul Shinmun*, June 13, 1995 (in Korean).

[10] "President Kim's Congratulatory Speech on August 15" (Full Text) *Seoul Shinmun*, August 16, 1995 (in Korean).

[11] "Expert on North Korea—Selig S. Harrison's Report on the Recent Situation in North Korea," *Chung-ang Ilbo*, September 28, 1995 (in Korean).

[12] See Kurata, op cit., p. 256.

THE UNITED STATES AND JAPAN: SECURITY RELATIONS IN TOMORROW'S ASIA

WILLIAM CLARK, JR.

"To maintain the [security] alliance, which is desirable, requires restoring political dialogue. Yet when it comes to Japanese culture, producing dialogues of any kind is not exactly an easy assignment. The Japanese communicate by creating a mood. We [the United States] communicate by asking direct questions."[1]

This quotation captures, with brief clarity, the difficulties facing the U.S.–Japan security alliance as it enters a critical period of redefinition. The mood in both countries has changed forever; the old conceptual framework for maintaining this vital alliance no longer fits well. During the era of containment, important and tangible foundations were laid for the evolving alliance mechanism. Both countries met their strategic objectives in the Cold War, and via this security relationship they established a strong position to address the difficult challenges that face the region today. Thus, while difficult questions are now emerging, they can be approached with confidence; the focus must now be on how to adapt to a rapidly changing environment, how to improve cooperation, and how to expand the role and mission of alliance partnership.

One of the most difficult questions is, as one observer wryly notes, "Can the world's largest debtor continue to guarantee the security of the world's largest creditor?"[2] Some assert that the clear paradigmatic shift, from the geo-strategic to the geo-economic, has been overplayed. It is apparent that any nation today with serious doubts about its domestic economic future will be forced to reassess or revamp its external security commitments to accommodate pressing internal needs.

With surprising speed following the end of the Cold War, the world has been challenged by political and military disputes that emerged from "suspended animation" to return to their historical norms. Forces of instability and uncertainty, held in check by a bipolar world dominated by a global containment strategy, are now accepted as part of the new order. Without a clear regional adversary, U.S. foreign policy makers continue to be uncertain over the merits of an "assertive" multilateralist or a "selective" unilateralist approach toward international engagement. As a result, the United States has had to work even harder to reassure its alliance partners that neo-isolationism will not overly influence its policy options.

KEY CONSIDERATIONS IN THE ASIA-PACIFIC REGION

Paradigms and policy debates aside, the basis for continuing the U.S.–Japan security alliance is clearer when the following changes facing the region are examined.

(1) The Soviet military threat has diminished; Russian expansionism is stalled at the moment.

(2) The U.S. military presence in Asia has yet to be modified to address new conditions.

(3) Relations between China and Russia have improved.

(4) Relations between China and the United States lack strategic direction.

(5) The Japanese economy is no longer the undisputed center of Asian growth; Japan remains, politically, a "status quo" power.

(6) China's regional and global economic influence will increase in the next century; China is a "dissatisfied" power.

(7) The Korean Peninsula will be reunified by early next century.

(8) Prospects for improved cross-strait political relations between China and Taiwan will continue to decline.

Given these changes, many Asian leaders fear a power vacuum in East Asia, one that will eventually be filled by actors other than the United States and Russia. Asian states, particularly those supporting a U.S. presence in the region, face the difficult task of lobbying for a continued U.S. forward deployed presence and at the same time of exploring a more self-reliant, post–Cold War regional diplomacy. A solid U.S. presence must still be based on existing alliances in Northeast Asia. The new regional diplomacy will have the greatest chance for success if it is based on the expansion of pre-existing U.S. bilateral security commitments.

Most Asian leaders continue to welcome a U.S. military presence in the region. Still, the changing nature of the challenges leads some actors to question the depth of a U.S. regional commitment absent the glue of the Cold War. Some currently seek other avenues to pursue their security objectives. Three factors regarding the future security environment of Asia complicate the equations:

(1) There is a wide diversity among Asian perceptions of regional security issues;

(2)   Lingering political suspicions continue to drive the region's push toward defense modernization; and

(3)   The new balance of power in Asia is far from clear.

CHINA—A MAJOR POWER

One issue that focuses much attention in Asia today, and is dealt with at greater length elsewhere in this study, is the re-emergence of China on the modern stage. All the nations on China's periphery have been aware of the power potential present in the 1.2 billion citizens of that nation. Until recently, however, because of failed policies at the center, the full impact of China has not been fully felt in Asian policy circles. Today, a newly assertive China has adopted policies that hold the promise of returning it to the position in Asia that it held for thousand of years—the biggest, strongest, and richest nation in the region. While it is doubtful that China today has any revanchist policies regarding Siberia, the new states of Central Asia, or in Southeast Asia, with the exception of disputed areas, it will expect respect from those around its borders as its rightful due. It is clearly not politically correct in Asia today to discuss China as a threat. It also makes no sense to talk in terms of "containing" China. At the same time, Japan and the United States will have to come to terms with this "new boy on the block." For Japan, the relationship will have the pitfalls of rekindling old rivalries. For the United States, the re-emergence of China will bring into even sharper focus the reality that, while the United States is in Asia because it wants to be and might withdraw, China is a constant in Asia that will not fade.

THE TAIWAN ISSUE

Flowing from China's new position is the increasing difficulty of addressing the Taiwan issue for both the United States and Japan. The recent flap over the visit to the United States of the President of the Republic of China is only the tip of the iceberg. For very different historical reasons, Japan and the United States both have obligations to Taiwan. At the same time, both must deal with an increasingly assertive China. Complicating the equation is the demographic shift in Taiwan, the move toward democracy, and the fading of the close family ties that once bound many on Taiwan to the mainland.

THE KOREAN PENINSULA—FUTURE PROSPECTS

The Korean Peninsula, also covered elsewhere in the study, is a critical factor in the formulation of future U.S.–Japan security policy— not as in the past, as a hot spot that might erupt into war at any given moment, but rather as a source of possible destabilization, refugee flows, and force structure reconfiguration. Reunification of the Korean Peninsula under one government will not be easy; nor will it be tidy. The confusion and economic dislocation that could ensue will stretch the abilities of the Government of the Republic of Korea and its friends and allies. Successful reunification in the longer term will pose important strategic considerations as well. Absent the threat from the North, the rationale for the stationing of U.S. ground forces on the peninsula will rapidly erode. The U.S.–Japan security arrangement will be even more defined in terms of aiding stability in Asia. The outlines of the revised rationale for continued cooperation are becoming clearer, and work should be started now to prepare for the adjustments that will be required.

ASIAN REGIONAL PROBLEMS

Tomorrow's Asia will have to revisit a variety of long-standing territorial disputes and at the same time address difficult new challenges, such as nuclear proliferation, nature-resource depletion, declining fisheries, overpopulation and migration, and transnational pollution. There are today promising regional fora that will someday mature and effectively address these issues. The U.S.–Japan security alliance can do much to assist in this process and, at a minimum, can provide the political coverage necessary to allow other fora to develop without being overwhelmed by these new challenges. The two most promising new regional institutions, the Asia-Pacific Economic Cooperation forum and the Association of Southeast Asian Nations Regional Forum, continue to count on the United States and Japan for quiet leadership. The alliance should not seek to find a new regional adversary in order to continue, but rather should take up these new challenges and opportunities. What the alliance does need is a modification in its structure and mission to accommodate the decline of the Soviet threat and the rise of multipolar security concerns. Fortunately, this is starting to happen.

In September 1995, Japanese Defense Minister Seishiro Eto and U.S. Secretary of Defense William Perry agreed to look into expanding U.S.–Japan military cooperation in U.N. peacekeeping. In particular, the two countries would consider extending the current Acquisition and Cross-Servicing Agreement (ACSA) to apply to Japanese peacekeeping activities. The United States has long stated its support for Japan's bid for U.N. Security Council membership and for increased Japanese participation in peacekeeping and humanitarian missions. Today, the security relationship requires that it be shaped by a dynamic rather than a static vision. The broadening of the security relationship to encompass global security objectives should not be at the expense of greater cooperation in the regional context. The challenges facing the two countries are equally compelling at both levels of policy analysis.

At the regional level, joint cooperation in disaster relief, environmental monitoring, and counter-proliferation are areas already in play. Cooperation in these areas not only bridges the bilateral and global dimensions of the relationship but adds a much needed regional focus. The Hanshin earthquake and Aum gas scare demonstrated a willingness in Japan to explore new roles for its Self Defense Forces. The U.S. military, which provided some assistance in both incidents, can find new areas for cooperation with their Japanese counterparts as both countries begin to explore greater cooperation regionally and globally.

Notes

[1] Henry Kissinger, *Reflections on U.S.–Asian Relations*, First Annual B.C. Lee Lecture, Heritage Foundation, February 1, 1995.

[2] Robert A. Manning, "Future Shock or Renewed Partnership? The U.S.–Japan Alliance Facing the Millennium," *The Washington Quarterly*, Autumn 1995, p. 87.

THE UNITED STATES AND JAPAN: SECURITY RELATIONS IN TOMORROW'S ASIA

KIYOFUKU CHUMA

U.S.–JAPAN RELATIONS NEED NO DRASTIC MEDICINE

The sweeping changes in the international environment brought about by the end of the Cold War continue to rock the U.S.–Japan relationship. While the Soviet Union was until recently the target of containment in the American global strategy and Japan's regional tactics, today Russia does not pose a threat of military confrontation. As a result, Japan's importance to the United States is no longer based on partnership in containing the Soviet Union.

During the Cold War, the United States was generous to Japan in many respects—in the political, economic, and security arenas—and obtained a forward base adjacent to the Soviet Union. This generosity was the result of American strategy during the early years of the Cold War, when the United States was willing to support any anti-communist government to prevent the so-called "domino effect," even at the expense of tolerating unfavorable factors, such as human right abuses. Just as the United States adjusted its view when it realized that the domino effect was an illusion, Washington is now changing its Japan policy in political, economic, and security terms because it perceives that its national interests are no longer served by being generous toward Japan. A typical example of this new view is to be found in an article by Chalmers Johnson and D.B. Keehn, "The Pentagon's Ossified Strategy," *Foreign Affairs*, July/August 1995.

Aside from the question of whether this view is right or wrong, it is very likely that it will become increasingly influential in the United States. Contrasting views, such as those of Joseph S. Nye, Jr., in "The Case for Deep Engagement" in the same issue of *Foreign Affairs*, also assume that U.S.–Japan relations will change, or that changes in the mutual security relationship are inevitable. Given the present American preoccupation with domestic affairs, one can expect the age of U.S.–Japan interdependence to come to a close in the near future.

Vehemently critical views of Japan, such as those expressed in the Chalmers Johnson article, are not useful for building constructive relations between the United States and Japan. Japanese should coolly discuss and refute such views, but so far this is not happening. One problem is that Japan lacks a definitive policy to cope with changes in U.S. attitudes and therefore has no means of its own to deal with them. Some senior officials in the Japanese government are displeased with Chalmers Johnson's provocative arguments, while others are relieved by the moderate stance taken by Joseph S. Nye, Jr. In any event, Japan has not yet made any serious effort to cope with the changing bilateral relationship —a state of affairs that is clearly recognized by both Johnson and Nye.

The three parties in Japan's coalition government—the Liberal Democratic Party, the Social Democratic Party, and the Sakigake Party —as well as the opposition Shinseito Party, all mouth slogans which firmly advocate maintaining the Japan–U.S. Security Treaty system, but they are all silent on details of how to handle changes in the U.S.–Japan relationship. It is ironic that the Social Democratic Party declared its support for maintaining the security treaty system at the very time that doubts about it were being raised in the United States. It seems that political problems are often left hanging in Japan without due responsibility being exercised to resolve them.

GAP IN SECURITY PERCEPTIONS BETWEEN THE UNITED STATES AND JAPAN

A serious problem has arisen in U.S.–Japan relations because of different security perceptions in the two countries. Both the quantity and quality of doubts and irritation have grown intense in the United States, causing some to wonder: "What is the Japanese perception of global security in the completely altered strategic environment following the end of the Cold War?" Doubts and irritation are growing in Japan as well about whether the United States is eager to guarantee Japan's security after the Cold War.

Making this situation even more difficult is the very sensitive nature of national security issues that confines such doubts and irritation to the realm of domestic politics in the two countries. The normal processes of an alliance include a frank interchange of news at the official level that is now missing. Frustration is growing for this reason, particularly in the United States.

The two countries' differences in perceptions of global security and of the U.S.–Japan security system in the post–Cold War era are summarized below:

Different Perceptions of the Threat

With the end of the Cold War, the focus of the security threat has become obscure. The United States is formulating its military strategy and organizing its military forces on the basis of a fluid strategic environment in which potential threats are perceived throughout the world. This thinking, with its global perspective, does not necessarily entail an unconditional commitment to defending U.S. allies. Japan, on the other hand, still perceives Russia, China, and North Korea as potential threats; it remains preoccupied with defending its borders, and it lacks the capacity to consider global security issues.

Different Perceptions of the U.S.–Japan Security Treaty

While Japan continues to emphasize Article 5 of the U.S.–Japan Security Treaty, which prescribes U.S.–Japan defense cooperation in case Japan is attacked, the United States is now emphasizing Article VI, which prescribes corresponding action in the event of an emergency somewhere in the Far East (or the Asia-Pacific region)—even if Japan itself were not attacked. Furthermore, misunderstandings arising from the one-sided character of the treaty (Japan's so-called "free ride") still prevail in the United States to such an extent that the true spirit of the security system is lost.

Different Perceptions of the U.S. Military Presence in Japan

The U.S. public and some members of the establishment believe that Japan should bear a larger proportion of the expenses for stationing U.S. military forces in Japan because they think that the purpose of these forces is to defend Japan. In contrast, while not denying this reasoning, the Japanese believe that the presence of U.S. forces in Japan contributes to U.S. national interests, and they perceive that they are stationed in Japan mainly for worldwide deployment, and not exclusively for deployment in the Asia-Pacific region.

Different Perceptions of the Right to Collective Self-Defense

Successive Japanese governments have claimed that exercising the right to collective self-defense would be unconstitutional. No doubt U.S. leaders are less than satisfied with this argument, but because only a minority of Japanese argue that the country's right to collective self-defense should be legitimized, it will be difficult to have the Japanese and Americans agree on this issue. Yet the United States and Japan might encounter an emergency situation at some point—for instance, a military conflict off the Korean Peninsula; we might then potentially see warships of the Japanese Maritime Self-Defense Force passively observing the operations of the U.S. forces without participating in the hostilities or providing support. Such a situation would be a nightmare.

THE INCREASINGLY IMPAIRED U.S.–JAPAN SECURITY SYSTEM

Although the differences in perceptions of the security system have impaired U.S.–Japan relations, neither side is prepared for the dramatic steps needed to remedy the situation. The two countries have left important issues unresolved and as a result some of the following problems have arisen.

- The United States expanded its perception of the implications of the U.S.–Japan Security Treaty beyond the framework of Article 5 (defense of Japan) and Article VI (defense of the Far East) to encompass global defense. This new perception is in conflict with the treaty and has weakened the authority of the treaty itself. Moreover, the agreement on the ratio at which the expenses of stationing U.S. troops in Japan is to be shared, prescribed in an agreement on these troops in the treaty, has become a dead letter because there is such a large gap between the provisions of the agreement and reality. While Japan increasingly complains about this matter, the United States is also complaining strongly as it asks why Japan cannot understand the nature of post–Cold War crises and why it cannot contribute funds for global security.

- After the Cold War ended, people in Japan, and particularly in Okinawa, expected U.S. bases to be reduced or eliminated as a peace dividend. They are disappointed because there has been no real change. The Japanese expect changes to be made in the deployment of U.S. forces as arrangements based on the Soviet threat are shifted to the security of the Asia-Pacific region. An explanation should be provided if there is to be no change in the deployment of military forces. There are also persistent complaints that Japan alone should not have to suffer from the pollution caused by the military bases, and that other countries should allow military bases for the security of the entire Asia-Pacific region.

The post–Cold War U.S. global strategy, which lacks transparency, is more important than the two foregoing problems. But a lack of clarity about it has invited speculation and anxiety among the Japanese. Recently, strong views are being expressed in Japan, particularly among defense specialists, that if U.S. strategy does not specify a threat, the United States cannot defend Japan in the event of an emergency, and that U.S. troops will sooner or later be withdrawn from Japan. As a result, the hasty argument has been advanced in Japan that the current security system is not a firm foundation for Japanese national security, and that Japan has no alternative but to develop its own defense capabilities. It should be noted that this situation strengthens advocates of self-sufficient defense capabilities who assert that they are ready to abandon the security treaty if this is followed by steps to strengthen independent defense capabilities. Their view of completely abolishing the security treaty corresponds curiously with the views of Chalmers Johnson and others who claim that this is a good idea.

AIMING FOR A NEW SECURITY TREATY

Abolition of the security treaty is drastic medicine that would worsen U.S.–Japan relations for three reasons. First, economic tensions between the two countries are already severe and are being steadily exacerbated by slow rates of economic growth and growing nationalism in both countries. Favorable political relations cannot be expected if both economic and security relations come under greater pressure.

The second reason is that expenditures to achieve self-sufficient defense capabilities would change Japan's economic structure, strengthen its defense industries, and invite full-scale arms exports that would have a great impact on the world arms market. But Japan cannot expect rapid growth in its gross national product, and its national budget will remain about the same size for some time. If a self-sufficient defense capacity had to be budgeted under these circumstances, contributions for U.S. troops stationed in Japan would have to decrease, and this would certainly affect the U.S. global strategy.

Finally, strengthening Japan's defense capacity would incite neighboring countries to increase their military forces as well, with the attendant risk of an unprecedented arms race developing in the Asia-Pacific region. Such a situation would not be good for regional peace, and the United States, which claims to be a balancing force in the region, would have difficulty positioning itself with respect to Japan and the other countries in the region. Tensions between Japan and the United States would inevitably grow.

WHAT IS A GOOD SOLUTION?

There is an old Japanese method for solving this kind of a problem. The story has it that a man found a wallet containing three ryo (an archaic Japanese currency unit), which he turned in to the police station. The policeman there called the owner, who declined to take the money, saying that it was no longer his and belonged instead to the man who had found it. The finder refused to take the money, claiming that it was not rightfully his either. In desperation, the policeman added one ryo from his own pocket and told the two men that the total of four ryo would be shared equally between the two: the finder would lose one ryo of what he found, the owner would lose one ryo of what he originally had, and the policeman would lose one ryo as well. Thus, everyone would suffer an equal loss.

The United States, Japan, and other countries in the Asia-Pacific region should adopt this type of spirit. Each should understand the situation of the others and make concessions to achieve world security in the post–Cold War era. The following are some suggestions toward this end.

- Both Japan and the United States should admit that the purpose and spirit of the U.S.–Japan Security Treaty have changed. Therefore they should review the Treaty and attempt to create a progressive alliance for the 21st century, with the aim of completing their work by the year 2000. Such an alliance should emphasize security protection and conflict prevention for the Asia-Pacific region as a whole and should not be addressed to any specific threat. While the alliance should start as a bilateral arrangement, it could become a multilateral framework in the future and include Japan's neighbors at their request.

- U.S. military forces should be deployed in the Asia-Pacific region as long as they are required by countries in the region. To this end, Japan should accept that U.S. forces will continue to be stationed in Japan and should bear the naval supply and repair expenses for the Seventh Fleet. At the same time, other countries in the Asia-Pacific region should accept redeployment of U.S. forces so that base pollution would be shared equitably. In particular, it would be effective to shift the Marine Corps forces now based in Okinawa to countries belonging to the Association of Southeast Asian Nations so that the forces could monitor both the Asia-Pacific and the Middle East regions.

- As for the expenses of U.S. troop deployment, a council should be set up by Japan, the United States, and the Asia-Pacific countries to negotiate the issue. Countries in the region should contribute part of their wealth from economic growth to support U.S. troops as a cost of national security. As part of a revised security relationship, Japan and the United States should also negotiate a bilateral agreement redefining how the costs of their respective contributions to regional security are to be shared. Americans should understand that the U.S. military presence in the Asia-Pacific region benefits not only other countries but also their own interests and should no longer accuse Japan and other Asian countries of enjoying a "free ride" by accepting the presence of U.S. forces.

- Finally, the most difficult issue is China's position in the Asia-Pacific region. China will certainly become the largest Asian power in the 21st century in terms of its economic and military capability, although opinions vary about the speed at which this will happen. Future security in Asia cannot be managed without comprehensively considering China's role. The United States should have a military presence in the Asia-Pacific region to play fully the role of a balancing force, preventing Chinese hegemony by making full use of peaceful and diplomatic methods. The United States and China should conclude a security or peace and friendship treaty to enhance friendly economic relations; and Japan, the United States, and China should support a U.S.–China relationship that is free of military rivalry.

BEYOND EXTENDED DETERRENCE: POLICIES FOR THE ASIAN THEATER

SPURGEON M. KEENY

A THEATER MISSILE DEFENSE SYSTEM?

The Japanese government is currently considering whether to deploy a national ballistic missile defense system in cooperation with the United States. In making this decision, Japan should weigh the actual need for such a system, taking into account its negative political and security consequences as well as its high cost. This judgment demands a critical assessment of the nature of the threats Japan faces and the impact of a decision to deploy on regional and global perceptions of Japan's intentions, taking into account the increasingly controversial nature of the U.S. ballistic missile defense program with which Japan would be closely associated.

As part of its "counter-proliferation" strategy, the United States is pursuing a major program to develop and deploy theater missile defense (TMD) systems to protect U.S. forces and allies from ballistic missiles with ranges of up to 3,500 kms. In support of the program, U.S. officials assert that 15 to 20 nations have or will soon have ballistic missiles and that "more than 25 countries, many of them adversaries of the United States, possess or may be developing nuclear, chemical, or biological weapons."

U.S. critics of the TMD program argue that the "threat" is grossly exaggerated because most of the countries included are not potential adversaries, will only have short-range (less than 1,000 km) missiles for the foreseeable future, and do not have ongoing nuclear weapons programs. In fact, Saudi Arabia is the only non-nuclear weapon state with missiles in the 3,500 km range, and these were purchased eight years ago from China, which has now accepted the export constraints of the Missile Technology Control Regime (MTCR). Consequently, the rationale for the U.S. TMD program appears to be built on the unlikely assumption that both the nuclear non-proliferation and MTCR regimes will fail catastrophically in the not too distant future.

To counter the postulated theater missile threat, the United States is pursuing several programs, including: the land-mobile Theater High-Altitude Area Defense (THAAD) system, which can cover a large region against missiles with 3,500 km range, and upper- and lower-tier ship-based systems with even greater technical capabilities. If deployed in Japan, either THAAD or the Navy's upper-tier system could provide full national coverage of Japan. The actual effectiveness of the defense, however, remains unproven and to some extent unprovable.

The U.S. TMD program has become a major policy issue between the United States and Russia because both THAAD and the Navy upper tier system have sufficient capability to violate the Anti-Ballistic Missile (ABM) Treaty as traditionally interpreted. The United States has unsuccessfully attempted to obtain Russian agreement on a treaty "clarification" that would permit these and even more powerful systems. However, even if Russian agreement were obtained, the prospect of large-scale U.S. and Russian deployment of high performance land-, sea-, and air-based TMD systems that could provide a nationwide ballistic missile defense would probably prevent further reductions in U.S. and Russian strategic forces below the START II levels, and might prevent Russian ratification of START II.

Current efforts by the Republican Congressional majority to mandate the deployment of a full national ballistic missile defense has further imperiled the ABM Treaty. If this policy prevails, prospects for reductions below START II levels are essentially nil, and START II, and even START I, would be imperiled. In submitting START II to the Russian parliament, President Boris Yeltsin made clear that ratification should be contingent on the continuation of the ABM Treaty. Failure to continue the strategic nuclear arms reduction process would be widely seen as a repudiation of the political commitments made by the nuclear weapon states in obtaining approval for the indefinite extension of the NPT.

In assessing the ballistic missile threat to Japan, the only countries that pose even a hypothetical threat today or for the foreseeable future are Russia, North Korea, and China.

Russia, which the United States no longer considers a nuclear adversary, can hardly be considered a ballistic missile threat to Japan. As a consequence of the Intermediate Nuclear Forces (INF) Treaty, Russia does not have any land-based ballistic missiles with ranges between 500-3,500 km, against which the theater missile defenses are supposed to operate. More fundamentally, Russia does not have any interests in the Far East that could conceivably cause it to launch, or threaten to launch, intercontinental ballistic missile (ICBM) or submarine-launched ballistic missile (SLBM) forces against a non-nuclear Japan.

THE NORTH KOREA RATIONALE

The most frequent public rationale for a Japanese missile defense has been the threat of North Korean nuclear-armed ballistic missiles. However, given the recent success of the efforts to contain and then eliminate the North Korean nuclear weapons program, it now seems unlikely this threat will eventuate. Japan is working closely with the United States and South Korea to implement the U.S.–North Korean Agreed Framework, which is on schedule and shows every indication of eventual success. With the elimination of North Korea's nuclear weapon program and its gradual entry into the international community, Pyongyang will also probably be persuaded to abandon its ballistic missile program. But, even if the program continues, it will hardly pose a serious threat to Japan with conventional warheads. Moreover, the notion cannot be taken seriously that North Korea would seek to intimidate Japan with a few ballistic missiles possibly armed with one or two nuclear warheads secretly fabricated from unaccounted-for fissile material. The suggestion that a future reunited Korea will emerge as a nuclear threat to Japan is so unlikely and so far in the future that it should not be a factor in a current decision to deploy a ballistic missile defense.

China poses the only credible ballistic missile threat to Japan. Under the U.S. nuclear umbrella, Japan has lived comfortably with this threat for the last 30 years, which included periods of much greater tension and ideological confrontation than exist today. China would certainly not undertake an act that would invite a U.S. or Russian nuclear response. Beyond this, in the absence of future Japanese aggression, which is most unlikely, there does not appear to be any situation where China would use, or threaten to use, nuclear-armed ballistic missiles against Japan, even in the absence of a U.S. nuclear guarantee.

Although the Chinese ballistic missile force is relatively small (about 100 land-based ballistic missiles with ranges between 1,800-5,000 km and 24 submarine-based missiles with ranges of about 1,700 km), an effective national defense of the entire Japanese homeland would still be a substantial undertaking. A truly nationwide defense employing a layered land-based system such as THAAD, a two-tiered sea-based system, or some combination of the two could cost as much as $20 billion. To take this defensive mission seriously, Japan also would have to deploy comparably expensive defenses against theater range aircraft, which the Chinese have, and sophisticated cruise missiles, which are certainly within future Chinese technical capabilities.

POLITICAL AND STRATEGIC COSTS

While the costs and technology of these systems are certainly within Japanese capabilities, the larger political and strategic costs would appear to argue strongly against such a decision. These costs would include the perceived signal to other countries in the area, particularly China, that Japan intended to take an active military role in the area, using this defensive system as a protective shield under which it could engage in future power projection without fear of retaliation. This after all is the underlying rationale advanced by the United States for its massive TMD deployment. China would certainly see this defense as specifically aimed at it, since these defenses have been designed against a 3,500 km range threat, which is the range of the Chinese CSS-2 missile. China might also conclude that as part of this military buildup, Japan would in due course decide to develop nuclear weapons. These concerns would stimulate the Chinese to increase their ballistic missile force and other nuclear delivery systems to assure continued Japanese vulnerability to the Chinese nuclear deterrent.

More generally, a Japanese missile defense deployment decision would raise concerns throughout Asia and the Pacific as to long-term Japanese intentions. A Japanese commitment to such a defense, which would be widely seen as reflecting Japanese belief that the nuclear non-proliferation regime will inevitably fail, could fuel regional and international speculation that Japanese interest in the plutonium fuel cycle was simply a stepping stone to a major nuclear weapons capability. Critics would inevitably argue that Japan would soon decide that an independent nuclear weapons capability, for which Japanese civilian plutonium is readily available, would provide a far better and less expensive deterrent to foreign nuclear threats than any missile defense system.

Intimate Japanese involvement in a program that would be seen by many, including Russia, as violating the ABM Treaty could seriously undermine Japan's position as an international leader in efforts to eliminate nuclear weapons. If the U.S. position on TMD and a nationwide anti-ballistic missile system leads to the loss of START II, and possibly of START I, as well as prevents further progress on reduction of strategic nuclear arms, the international community will severely criticize the United States for violating its political commitments in obtaining the indefinite extension of the NPT. Although Japan is not itself a party to the ABM Treaty, by deploying a national ballistic missile defense, it would be seen as sharing responsibility with the United States for the collapse of the strategic arms reduction regime and for endangering the nuclear non-proliferation regime.

Finally, there is the question of Japan's relations with the United States, which is currently encouraging Japan to deploy cooperatively a Japanese version of THAAD and/or the two-tiered navy system. Whether the U.S. interest is intended to promote broader Japanese defense burden-sharing in East Asia or simply to gain financial support for the extremely expensive U.S. TMD, program is not clear. In the long term, such a Japanese deployment could facilitate a withdrawal of U.S. forces as well as U.S. nuclear guarantees. Japan's larger interest would appear to be to maintain a guaranteed U.S. nuclear deterrent and to be able to call on the mobile U.S. TMD systems in the extremely unlikely situation that they were ever needed. For its part, the United States could hardly fault Japan for relying on the U.S. nuclear deterrent and U.S. TMD systems, which are being developed to provide protection to U.S. allies overseas.

When all aspects of the issue are taken into account, Japan's long-term security interests would appear to be best served by rejecting a commitment to any missile defense system that would be widely seen not only as unnecessarily undermining prospects for further reductions in strategic nuclear arms but also as a de-stabilizing new element in the strategic balance in East Asia.

BEYOND EXTENDED DETERRENCE:
POLICIES FOR THE ASIAN THEATER

AKIO WATANABE

The basic assumption of the argument made here is that both the United States and Japan are interested in upholding and strengthening the Nuclear Non-Proliferation Treaty (NPT) regime as a means to achieving the long-term goal of a world free of nuclear weapons. But many uncertainties about the future course of government policies in both countries as well as in the international environment might cause some intra-alliance discord over NPT-related issues in the years ahead. The policy of the current U.S. administration is fluid; it reflects the delicate balance of power between two different schools of thought in policy circles about the role of nuclear weapons following the dissolution of the Soviet Union and other post–Cold War strategic changes: nuclear marginalization vs. traditionalism.

JAPAN'S NPT POLICY

Japan's official policy, especially since the Hosokawa government, reflects a firm commitment to the goals of the NPT, despite considerable hesitation before the decision was reached. But Japan's commitment remains contingent on certain things, the most important being the future direction of U.S. policy, which in turn depends on a number of variable factors both inside and outside the United States.

The Japanese government's commitment to the NPT is based on its belief in three major factors: (1) the pledge of the existing nuclear powers in Article VI of the Treaty to phase out their own nuclear weapons; (2) the U.S. pledge that it will maintain its nuclear umbrella over allies until nuclear disarmament is achieved; and (3) the assurance in the NPT concerning the right of non-nuclear nations to carry out peaceful nuclear programs. These are issues over which lengthy debates were conducted over six years, between 1970 and 1976—from the time that Japan signed the NPT until it was ratified.

The debates over NPT ratification in the 1970s provide the political and intellectual contours for the recent debates in Japan over the extension of the NPT regime. Important changes have occurred in the intervening period. First, the end of the Cold War has given rise to new thinking in the United States about nuclear strategy, exemplified by ideas such as "minimal deterrence," "conventional deterrence," and "nuclear marginalization." Developments such as the Intermediate Nuclear Forces (INF) Treaty in 1987, the Strategic Arms Reduction Treaty I (START I) in 1991, START II in 1993, and other initiatives taken individually or jointly by the former Soviet Union and the United States in recent years have helped to enhance the credibility of Article VI of the NPT.

Second, the Japanese government has been firmly committed to a policy favoring nuclear power programs and has gone a long way toward implementing this policy. The policy is based on the NPT's stipulation of the "inalienable rights" of the treaty signatories to use nuclear materials for peaceful purposes. Thus, despite the technical distinction in the Treaty between nuclear and non-nuclear nations, the NPT has not interfered with the freedom of the Japanese authorities and experts in the field of nuclear-power programs to develop Japan's nuclear-power capabilities for peaceful purposes.

Given these factors, the ambivalent attitude of the Japanese toward the NPT extension issue in 1995 was difficult for many outside observers to understand. A possible explanation was the still lingering suspicion that the Japanese have over assurances by the nuclear weapon states in two areas. The first is their pledge of nuclear disarmament, and the second is the NPT guarantee of non-discriminatory treatment and inalienable rights of all signatories to use nuclear materials for peaceful purposes. One can say that the issues that arose in the earlier debates over NPT ratification have not been completely put to rest. Nevertheless, the relative ease with which the Japanese government reached a final decision in favor of the NPT extension indicated changed conditions that affected the balance of power between the pro and con forces in the domestic debate over the issue.

IMPACT OF THE END OF THE COLD WAR

It is ironic that the end of the Cold War has brought forth new problems about NPT-related issues in general and U.S.–Japanese relations over nuclear policy in particular. As long as Japan could rely on the U.S. nuclear umbrella, and as long as Japan could pursue its cherished nuclear energy programs, the Japanese could feel that their basic national interests were secure, while eventual nuclear disarmament would remain purely academic. The seeming harmony among the three factors underlying the Japanese policy referred to earlier has begun to be called into question with the advent of post–Cold War movements for a nuclear-free world. The Japanese should, of course, have no reason at all for lamenting these new movements.

The problem for now is not whether, but how to go from here to there. In this respect, potential tensions exist between the first and third policy factors as well as between the first and second. The first area of tension is related to increasing pressure from some quarters in the United States for completely dismantling Japanese energy programs that rely significantly on plutonium. The critics argue that a total ban on plutonium, whether for military or non-military use, is an essential part of the NPT regime. The second area of tension is over the apparent decreased credibility of the extended deterrence of the United States for the defense of its allies.

One of the possible consequences of the U.S. pursuit of a "nuclear marginalization" policy would be lowered credibility in its willingness and capability to protect its allies from attack by hostile nations using weapons of mass destruction (WMDs). This will create a new type of problem for the U.S.–led alliance system. A similar credibility problem about the U.S. nuclear umbrella existed during the Cold War, but it was not regarded as very important, especially in East Asia.

As long as uncertainties about Russia's future nuclear policy continue, U.S. proponents of nuclear marginalization will not be able to gain a complete upper hand over the traditionalists. The latter group will not be convinced by the argument that extended deterrence is obsolete because the United States and its allies no longer face a potential aggressor armed with nuclear bombs. In this sense, the Russian factor will continue to be a bone of contention between the traditionalists and marginalists in the future debate on the role of extended deterrence in the post–Cold War era.

UNCERTAINTIES ABOUT ASIAN REGIONAL POWERS

More important for the Asian theater, however, are the great uncertainties about the nuclear policies of regional powers like North Korea and China. Doubts about North Korea's nuclear weapons program have not yet been totally dispelled, despite the agreement reached on the Korean Peninsula Energy Development Organization (KEDO). It is also believed that Pyongyang already possesses a number of medium-range ballistic missiles as well as chemical and biological weapons. Thus, one of the challenges the U.S.–Japan alliance now faces is the question of how to deal with WMDs in the hands of a very unreliable regime in North Korea.

The first priority should, of course, be given to non-proliferation of the WMDs. Since some proliferation has already occurred, we must have some means to deal with those WMDs, nuclear or conventional. We should also have some means to stop further proliferation of WMDs by regimes like those in Pyongyang.

COUNTER-PROLIFERATION CONCEPT

This leads us to "counter-proliferation," a new and still loosely defined concept embracing a variety of measures designed to counter the threat of nuclear weapons through non-nuclear means.

In announcing the U.S. Defense Counterproliferation Initiative on December 7, 1993, the late Secretary of Defense Les Aspin described it as basically "an effort to develop new capabilities to deal with the growing threat of proliferation. We have to plan to fight wars different-ly. . . . For example, we're looking at improving non-nuclear penetrating munitions to deal with underground installations. We're working hard on better ways to hunt mobile missiles. And of course . . . we have reori-ented the Strategic Defense Initiative into the Ballistic Missile Defense Organization, focusing on the response to theater missile threats."

It is important to realize that technologically this concept, of which a Theater Missile Defense (TMD) system is an important ingre-dient, is at best at a very underdeveloped stage. In political terms, uncer-tainty exists about whether this concept will be accepted by domestic and external audiences as "non-provocative conventional defense." Thus, nuclear deterrence will, for the time being, remain a major defense strategy during this transition period.

IMPLICATIONS FOR CHINA

China has responded rather sharply to the suggested development of TMD by the United States and Japan, and it is calling the TMD a violation of the Anti-Ballistic Missile (ABM) Treaty, to which it is not even a party. China also accuses Japan by saying that a country under the nuclear umbrella of another country is not entitled to criticize the nuclear policy of a neighboring state. Would China then prefer to see Japan removed from the American nuclear umbrella? Is it suggesting that Japan should come under the Chinese nuclear umbrella? Or do the Chinese want to have a nuclear balance with Japan? It is difficult to answer these questions, but it is crystal clear that China is firmly com-mitted to further upgrading of its nuclear arsenal, which it regards as the status symbol of a great power.

The nuclear strategy situation in East Asia is at present very murky. Given the many uncertainties at the present time, one essential role for the United States is to uphold the alliance system if only to pre-vent the situation from becoming more complex and uncontrollable. It is said that few issues in the history of nuclear policy have been more vexed than the credibility of the nuclear guarantees at the heart of the alliance network. The U.S.–Japan alliance has not been as vexed by this issue as the North Atlantic Treaty Organization (NATO) was during the Cold War. Using the "three non-nuclear principles," Japan could afford to pretend its own innocence about the business of nuclear deterrence. An irony is that NPT-related issues, including extended deterrence, have become a real test for the viability of the U.S.–Japan alliance *after* the Cold War.

II.

ASIAN ENERGY DEVELOPMENT AND NON-PROLIFERATION

WORKING GROUP II

Co-Chairmen
Victor Gilinsky and Hiroyoshi Kurihara

Makoto Ishii
Atsuyuki Suzuki

*William J. Dircks and Jessica Tuchman Mathews
prepared working papers but were unable
to attend the Tokyo meeting and did not
participate in the Working Group.*

ASIAN ENERGY DEVELOPMENT AND NON-PROLIFERATION

REPORT OF WORKING GROUP II

REACTOR-GRADE PLUTONIUM AND NUCLEAR WEAPONS

1. The participants agreed that as a technical matter, with some additional efforts, a country can produce nuclear weapons using any kind of plutonium, employing well-known technologies.

2. Japanese participants stated that the disadvantages of using reactor-grade plutonium in military production and in a military setting make it an unlikely candidate for weapon use by normal governments. They also stated that, for such a purpose, it would be necessary to have, in addition to the plutonium itself, a program to develop a set of warheads with reliable, known yields—as well as facilities designed to produce plutonium in production-line quantities much larger than those of a civilian nuclear-power program.

3. There was agreement among the participants that international controls such as IAEA safeguards should apply to any type of plutonium, since its production carries with it a possibility, however small, of manufacturing nuclear weapons. The participants further agreed that, besides IAEA safeguards, additional international measures for deterring diversion of plutonium to nuclear weapons should be considered and proposed by the international community.

4. Even in the case of reactor-grade plutonium, the working group favors measures to forestall the widespread dispersion of such plutonium in usable form.

All participants agreed that strengthening international and national control of the physical protection of plutonium is of the utmost importance due to the possible risks of the diversion of plutonium by sub-national groups such as international terrorist groups.

PEACEFUL USES OF NUCLEAR ENERGY

1. The working group expressed the opinion that in future nuclear energy will be one of the important energy resources.

2. However, approaches to the further development of nuclear energy differ country by country. Japan wants to promote the recycling of nuclear fuel—that is, the utilization of plutonium in its civilian sector for reasons relating to its overall resource planning, environmental pro-

tection, and other factors. The United States does not promote the civilian use of plutonium for economic and non-proliferation reasons.

3. Japan has no intention of becoming a nuclear-weapon state. However, some experts in foreign countries have expressed their concern regarding Japanese intentions. Therefore, the Japanese participants pointed out, maintaining and strengthening the transparency and openness of the Japanese plutonium program is very important.

4. The U.S. participant stated that Japan has to consider seriously the influence of the Japanese plutonium program on the neighboring countries' nuclear programs.

Japanese participants expressed the view that the progress of the Japanese plutonium recycling program will not ultimately be a deciding factor in the neighboring countries' nuclear programs.

ASIAN NUCLEAR ENERGY DEVELOPMENT

1. The working group agreed that the world's major center of civilian nuclear power growth in the future will be Asia. Northeast Asian countries already have significant numbers of nuclear power stations. Southeast Asian countries could also emerge as states relying to a significant degree on civilian nuclear-power programs. A significant number of nuclear fuel-cycle facilities now exist in the Asian region.

2. The working group also agreed that the development of an Asian nuclear power organization (an ASIATOM) would be useful for the smooth development of nuclear energy in the region.

3. Possible elements of an ASIATOM could be the following:

- a regional safeguards system

- a regional nuclear fuel-cycle agency

- a nuclear-power safety regulatory system

- an organization for cooperation on research and development

The working group felt that the establishment and maintenance of an Asian regional safeguards system would be useful both for assisting safeguards implementation by the IAEA and as a significant regional confidence-building measure that could enhance regional stability.

With respect to the proposed fuel-cycle agency, the group agreed that regional treatment of spent-fuel management needs to be discussed further. There were diverse opinions concerning the desirability of a regional spent-fuel reprocessing center or enrichment center as part of a fuel-cycle agency. Some felt that it is too early to discuss such proposals seriously; others stated that such discussion should begin as soon as possible because development of the regional fuel-cycle concept would require a long preparatory period.

The working group agreed that nuclear-power safety and research and development are important and should be promoted.

4. Concerning the geographic extent of a possible ASIATOM, some participants thought that a Pacific Atomic Energy Community (PACATOM) concept (including Australia, the United States, and Canada) would be preferable; others expressed the opinion that the area for ASIATOM should be East and Southeast Asia, with South Asia not included, at least in the beginning, given the political complexities of that region. The participants considered the important issue of Chinese participation in a possible ASIATOM. The general view of the group was that, without the participation of China, the value of ASIATOM might be reduced drastically. Some participants, however, felt that China is too big to be accommodated as a single member of a regional framework.

REACTOR-GRADE PLUTONIUM: THE DEBATE OVER ITS MILITARY POTENTIAL

VICTOR GILINSKY

The basic security issue posed by the use of nuclear power to generate electricity is whether civilian nuclear-power programs contribute to the capability of developing nuclear weapons. In order to address this issue, it is necessary to consider two critical questions: Does a nuclear-power program reduce the effort and time that would be needed to make nuclear warheads? And if less time and effort would be needed, would this ease a possible decision to produce nuclear weapons?

IMPORTANCE OF NUCLEAR EXPLOSIVES

A useful starting point is the observation made by weapon scientists that the most difficult and time-consuming part of developing nuclear warheads is getting sufficient quantities of nuclear explosives. Without access to a military production program, would-be bomb makers may seek such materials, at least initially, from civilian stocks of plutonium and highly enriched uranium. International Atomic Energy Agency (IAEA) inspectors are intended to protect against this possibility.

Of the two possible nuclear explosives, plutonium is of most concern. The material forms in the reactor fuel during operation of uranium-fueled nuclear power reactors. A large power reactor can produce over 200 kg of plutonium per year whereas only about 5 kg are sufficient for a bomb. The world's power reactors annually produce perhaps 50 tons of plutonium. The amounts produced are so staggering when expressed in military terms that we have to check ourselves: Are we really talking about material that is useful for bombs? If we are, we obviously have a very serious security problem.

The security problem is far greater if its owners extract the plutonium—initially embedded in the reactor's highly radioactive spent fuel—by means of spent-fuel reprocessing. Once the plutonium is separated in the course of reprocessing, it can be put to military use quickly. At least that is so if we make the worst-case assumption that the country in question has previously done its bomb homework outside the purview of international inspectors. That this is plausible is a lesson we have to draw from the recent experience with Iraq.

Consider a situation when a country is no longer constrained by lack of nuclear explosives and can make bombs quickly. In these circumstances, IAEA inspections, even if they work as intended, no longer serve as a deterrent. That is, they can no longer reliably warn of misappropriation of nuclear material in time to affect the outcome. The situation then becomes similar to one in which the IAEA keeps track of the nuclear weapons themselves. It would be nice to periodically hear from Vienna about where the warheads are. But their inspection would not protect against their use if the owners decided to use them. Similarly, while it is true that almost all owners of commercial plutonium intend to use it as reactor fuel, it is also true that intentions can change. It is difficult to imagine how we can reliably protect against the misuse of all of the nuclear explosive capability around the world.

"REACTOR-GRADE" PLUTONIUM

Is this picture of the dangers of plutonium use overdrawn? Not everyone accepts that power-reactor plutonium, so-called "reactor-grade," is useful for military warheads. Indeed, insistence that it is not is a vital part of the rationale of plutonium's commercial use. Even the IAEA has been ambivalent. From the beginning, mainly on the basis of U.S. advice, the IAEA has formally assumed that all types of plutonium can be used for weapons, and it has treated them the same. In practice, the top IAEA inspectors did not fully trust U.S. advice, and they rationalized their weak inspection system accordingly. In part this was because the U.S. advice was (for security reasons) not adequately supported by technical information.

The technical justification for doubting the usefulness of reactor-grade plutonium for weapons is based on the much higher admixture of various plutonium isotopes (some slightly heavier kinds of plutonium) in this material than in the ideal weapon plutonium. This comes about because the uranium fuel rods in power reactors are subjected to much higher neutron irradiation than those in military plutonium production reactors. During the Manhattan Project, U.S. scientists discovered that the unwanted plutonium isotopes could reduce the likely explosion of the first warheads to what was called the "fizzle yield." (The fizzle yield was still about one kiloton.) Since then, the idea has frequently surfaced that anything but "weapon-grade" plutonium was not really useful for warheads and did not need the same protection.

ATOMS FOR PEACE

In launching the Atoms for Peace program in 1953, President Eisenhower said that "scientists" would render the plutonium in international commerce unsuitable for military use. In subsequent negotiations, Secretary of State John Foster Dulles was surprised to hear from Soviet Foreign Minister Vyacheslav Molotov that the Atoms for Peace program would spread the capabilities for war. He was even more surprised to hear from his assistant, Gerald Smith, that Molotov was right.

Once the international nuclear program was under way, it was too late to rethink plutonium use—or so many people thought. The world's nuclear programs were nearly all based on the notion that plutonium from current reactors would fuel future "fast-breeder" reactors that would ultimately take over the world's electric power generation. Plutonium use was legitimized by the new idea of IAEA inspection. If one worried about the shaky inspection system, it helped to believe that reactor-grade plutonium from current reactors was not really suitable for weapons anyway. (That fast-breeder reactors would produce lots of weapon-grade plutonium was left as a problem for the future.)

In 1976, I visited both IAEA officials in Vienna and German officials in Bonn responsible for the then-current German-Brazilian nuclear deal, which included reprocessing technology. In Vienna, the IAEA Director General surprised me by asking whether it was really true that one could make bombs with reactor-grade plutonium. He told me that some of his top people thought otherwise. Later, the top German official told me that his experts had assured him that the plutonium to be separated in Brazil was not weapon-usable. When I returned to Washington, I suggested that the United States provide briefings for these and other international officials. I attended the briefing for the IAEA Director General and saw him taken by complete surprise when a Livermore laboratory briefer said that the reactor-grade plutonium could be used for making warheads.

TECHNICAL FACTS AND THEIR SIGNIFICANCE

Weapon scientists say that not only can the reactor-grade plutonium be used for warheads, it can be used in high-performance warheads, including thermonuclear warheads. The popular view that envisions severely degraded performance for warheads based on reactor-grade plutonium is based on World War II technology. That has long been superseded and is no longer a limitation. To use reactor-grade plutonium takes some additional effort, not proportionately great, in directions that have to be pursued anyhow to accomplish the purpose with pure material. Whether the reactor-grade material would be used depends in part on the available alternatives. My view is that if reactor-grade plutonium had been the only nuclear explosive available over the past fifty years, the history of nuclear arms would not have been much different.

Still, to varying degrees, other alternatives are available, which leads to a more sophisticated question. Accepting the fact that reactor-grade plutonium can be used to make high-performance warheads, are not the difficulties of using it in military production such that, as a practical matter, it would never be used for military warheads? And, does this not mean the material is not a proliferation risk?

It is true that the greater radiation level and heat output of reactor-grade material make it less desirable than weapons-grade nuclear material for making nuclear weapons. One can get around the technical difficulties that these pose. Nevertheless, it does not seem plausible that a country would use reactor-grade plutonium for advanced warheads once a country has reached that stage of nuclear development. By the time it got these, it would likely have secured a source of plutonium (or highly enriched uranium) of preferable quality. For advanced states seeking nuclear weapons, reactor-grade plutonium's importance is as a transitional nuclear explosive, useful in getting a quick start in the nuclear weapons business. The ease of this option could affect crisis decisions to manufacture nuclear bombs. The principal deterrent to misappropriating reactor-grade plutonium for bombs, for a country eager to do so, is the uncertainty about other states' reactions. This is especially so during the interval of greatest vulnerability—between a country's evident decision to make bombs and having them in hand. If such a country must first extract the plutonium from radioactive spent fuel, the vulnerable interval and the deterrent effect are substantially increased.

CAN WE DISCRIMINATE?

This leaves us with the question: Is it necessary to subject peaceful and responsible countries to restrictions on plutonium use? Is it not more realistic to exempt the major industrial states from such restrictions, in particular the so-called industrial democracies with "good proliferation credentials"? There is some irony in such a suggestion from states that themselves criticize the current inequities in the Non-Proliferation Treaty's distinction between nuclear-weapon states and other states. It is not realistic to expect such a discriminatory agreement to stand up. Either we will have a system of common standards or we will have uncontrolled access to plutonium.

The recent suggestions for making civilian plutonium programs "transparent" and restricting stockpiling are steps in the right direction. But there is something self-contradictory about them, too. These proposals acknowledge, in effect, that the plutonium is dangerous because it could be used for bomb making. Otherwise, whey worry about whether there is a surplus? But if the materials are indeed dangerous because of their potential use for weapons, then the no-stockpiling plan does not deal with the problem adequately. The reason is that the amounts needed for substantial weapon stocks are, comparatively speaking, small enough that they would always be on hand, even under a "no stockpiling" plan.

CONCLUDING COMMENTS

What can we do about the possible destructive potential of reactor-grade plutonium? As long as we do not have effective means of protecting the plutonium around the world from bomb making, we should try to keep the technological barriers in place. The only way to keep these barriers up in places we worry about is also to accept them as a universal norm. That is why after careful study in 1976, President Gerald Ford moved the U.S. nuclear-power program away from reliance on plutonium. (President Jimmy Carter is mistakenly given the credit and blame for this major step.) Since then, the economic incentives for plutonium have diminished substantially, making the arguments for this course even more persuasive. President Ford said that nuclear energy has an important part to play in future energy generation, and it can play that role without undermining our security. That is still good advice.

REACTOR-GRADE PLUTONIUM: THE DEBATE OVER ITS MILITARY POTENTIAL

HIROYOSHI KURIHARA

Nuclear weapons require plutonium (Pu) and/or uranium (U) as fissile materials. The plutonium required has to be weapon-grade plutonium, for which there are dedicated military nuclear reactors (production reactors) in the nuclear-weapons state. For the peaceful uses of nuclear energy, such as for generation of electric power, uranium is the major fuel used. Plutonium is produced in the core of nuclear reactors. The ratio of various isotopes of plutonium, Pu-238 to Pu-242, is different, based on the type of nuclear power reactor and burn-up, among other factors. Light-water reactors (LWRs) are the major commercially used reactors in the world. The plutonium they produce has a fairly different ratio of isotopes than the plutonium produced by military production reactors. The plutonium produced in commercial reactors in the civilian sector is known as reactor-grade plutonium.

The isotopic compositions of various grades of plutonium are:

Weapon grade: 94% Pu-239, 6% Pu-240, (0.35% Pu-241)

Reactor grade: 1% Pu-238, 60% Pu-239, 24% Pu-240,
(LWR)   9% Pu-241, 5% Pu-242

MOX grade: 2% Pu-238, 40% Pu-239, 32% Pu-240, 18%
              Pu-241, 8% Pu-242

Other types of civilian reactors, such as gas-cooled reactors (GCRs, with average burn-up of 3,000 MWth-d/kg U) or heavy-water reactors (HWRs, with burn-up of 7,500 MWth-d/kg U) have different ratios of isotopic compositions. According to one expert, these are:[1]

HWR: 67% Pu-239, 27% Pu-240, 5% Pu-241, 1% Pu-242
GCR: 80% Pu-239, 17% Pu-240, 3% Pu-241, (0.3% Pu-242).

PRODUCTION OF NUCLEAR WEAPONS
USING REACTOR-GRADE PLUTONIUM

There are continuing discussions in the international community on whether reactor-grade plutonium can be used in the manufacture of nuclear weapons or nuclear explosive devices. Reactor-grade plutonium has a much higher ratio of minor isotopes like Pu-240 than weapon-grade plutonium. Therefore, it poses a significant level of risk of pre-initiation and significant risks of damaging important parts of weapons by decay heat; it also poses radiation health hazards to workers. Some argue that nuclear weapons cannot be manufactured using reactor-grade plutonium or that the disadvantages make it almost impossible. Others argue that such disadvantages can be solved by advanced technological methods.

The following discussion on "criticality," pre-initiation, and damage caused by decay heat and radiation has been assisted by the meeting of the Advisory Committee on the Explosive Properties of Reactor-Grade Plutonium held in conjunction with the third meeting of the Study Group on June 1, 1996. The members of this group were Victor Gilinsky; Michael May, former director of the Livermore Laboratory; and Harold Agnew, former director of the Los Alamos Laboratory, on the American side; and myself, Ryukichi Imai, and Atsuyuki Suzuki on the Japanese side.

CRITICALITY PROPERTIES OF REACTOR-GRADE PLUTONIUM

The critical mass of plutonium varies by the types of plutonium isotopes. Isotopes Pu-239 and Pu-241 are "fissile" material; fission reaction may be initiated by neutrons of any energy, whether slow (thermal) or fast. On the other hand, Pu-238, Pu-240, and Pu-242 are "fissionable" material; only neutrons with energy above some threshold can induce fission. For Pu-240, the fission threshold is close to 1 MeV, but above this the fission cross-section is larger than that of U-235 (fissile material). The bare critical mass of Pu-240 in a phase metal is about 40 kg, less than that of U-235 (52 kg in 94% enriched). (The bare critical mass of a material at standard density is the critical mass with no neutron reflector present.) Pu-242 and Americium (Am)-241, a decay product of Pu-241, have a fission threshold close to 1 MeV. The bare critical masses of these isotopes are about 100 kg.

The bare critical masses are not those one would need to construct a device, since by using a reflector a few inches thick, the critical mass of each of these materials can be reduced by a factor of two or so below the bare critical mass. However, the relative ranking of the critical masses will be preserved very nearly as reflectors are applied.

Most civilian nuclear power stations (LWR, HWR, and GCR) at present use thermal (slow) neutrons for chain reactions in the core. The nuclear fission reaction in these cores is made only by Pu-239 and Pu-241. The one exception is the fast-breeder reactor (FBR) for which the fast neutron is also used. But there are only a few such FBRs in the world. Spent fuel from such FBRs is not yet considered usable in the commercial sector. However, plutonium from the FBR core could be more abundant in the isotope of Pu-240, since the burn-up would be very high, and that would make it less attractive for weapon production. By contrast, material in the outer "blanket" of FBRs, mostly consisting of U-238, could produce weapon-grade plutonium and must be carefully watched. It should be emphasized that all isotopes of plutonium, whether fissile or fissionable, can be used for a nuclear explosion.

DEGRADATION OF YIELD BY PRE-INITIATION

According to a definitive study by J.C. Mark, if reactor-grade plutonium is substituted for weapon-grade plutonium in any nuclear device, the probability of detonation with an expected yield would be reduced. Typically, the yield would be reduced in range from one to a few times larger than the fizzle yield, which is the smallest yield that the assembly system can provide. However, its destructive power would still be large enough. If one used 7-8 kg reactor-grade plutonium, the fizzle yield would be up to 0.6 kilotons TNT, an explosive power that cannot be easily disregarded.

EFFECT OF DECAY HEAT AND RADIATION

Weapon-grade plutonium generates about 2.5 watts per kg, while reactor-grade plutonium generates more than 10.5 watts per kg. Since the high explosives around the plutonium core would have insulating properties, only 10 cm of such material could produce an equilibrium temperature in the core of about 190° C. The rate of chemical deterioration of many types of high explosives begins to be significant above about 100° C.[2]

As for emitted radiation, Jon Swarn of Chalmers University in Gotsborg, Sweden, has developed data indicating that the surface dose rate of material such as reactor-grade plutonium is about six times larger (and mixed plutonium-and-uranium oxide [MOX]-grade over eight times larger) than that of weapon-grade plutonium.[3]

The design of a crude explosive device using reactor-grade plutonium would certainly have to take account of such heat problems and radiation exposure. But, according to American experts, these problems can be overcome. For example, by using aluminum, which has almost 1,000 times greater thermal conductivity, in a thermal bridge, the temperature increase induced by reactor-grade plutonium could be drastically reduced.

IAEA SAFEGUARDS

The IAEA does not differentiate its safeguards implementation to plutonium of any type or grade under its safeguards regime. In the case of uranium, IAEA safeguards implementation differs based on the U-235 concentration ratio (highly enriched uranium vs. low-enriched uranium). A significant quantity for plutonium, according to the IAEA safeguards glossary, is 8 kg for the total element, irrespective of its isotopic ratio. It is not known whether the IAEA may begin to consider application of different modes of safeguards implementation for weapon-grade and for reactor-grade plutonium.

CONCLUSIONS

1. Theoretically, there is no difficulty in producing a nuclear explosive device with any reactor-grade plutonium, using well-known technologies.

2. The disadvantages of using weapon-grade plutonium in a military production setting make it an unlikely candidate for weapons use by most governments, because one would need to produce a set of warheads with a reliable known yield and materials that can be turned out efficiently on a production line.

3. However, an international terrorist group acting alone or on behalf of a rogue state, with interest in the possible use of one or a very few devices, might weigh such considerations differently. Radiation exposure associated with fabrication, that might be unacceptable for a sustained operation, might not be an obstacle for a single operation.

4. The objective of international safeguards is to detect and/or deter any diversion of nuclear material by a state. The activity of subnational groups, such as terrorists, is not covered by IAEA safeguards; it is the responsibility of each nation. Each country should, therefore, establish and maintain a physical protection system that serves as the main instrument to prevent possible malignant activities. IAEA has established a set of guidelines on state physical protection activities, but responsibility for implementation rests with each state.

5. For the present, therefore, it is of utmost importance that international and national controls on physical protection be strengthened by, for example, upgrading international conventions and guidelines for use and storage of plutonium. However, there is not enough justification at present to change the current IAEA safeguards' implementation for different grades of plutonium.

6. In June 1994, U.S. Department of Energy Secretary Hazel O'Leary stated that the United States had conducted a nuclear test in 1962 using reactor-grade plutonium. The plutonium used for this test was donated by the United Kingdom. The Financial Times said, after Secretary O'Leary's statement, that the U.K. government believes that production of nuclear bombs using plutonium from civilian nuclear power reactors is extremely difficult. The newspaper also quoted comments made by a spokesman of the Department of Trade and Industry

that this test had proved that reactor-grade might possibly be used for explosive devices, but that no one seriously considers using it due to the practical difficulties in manufacturing. The newspaper pointed out that the plutonium used for the test had originated in military operations of the U.K. Atomic Energy Agency from the Calder Hall Reactor in Cambria.

7. While it is theoretically possible to use reactor-grade plutonium to produce nuclear explosive devices, it is doubtful that even an international terrorist group could do so, because that would require a range of technical expertise in many fields, including shock hydrodynamics, critical assemblies, chemistry, metallurgy, machining, electrical circuits, explosives, and health physics. Reactor-grade plutonium therefore is not an attractive material for the production of nuclear weapons, or even for the manufacture of crude nuclear explosive devices.

Notes

[1] J.C. Mark, "Explosive Properties of Reactor-Grade Plutonium," Science & Global Security, 1992, Vol. 3, pp. 1-13.

[2] Gerhard Locke, "Why Reactor-grade Plutonium is No Nuclear-Explosive Suitable for Military Devices." Workshop on the Disposition of Plutonium, Bonn, Germany, June 1992.

[3] Egbert Kankeleit, et al., Bericht zur Waffentanglichkeit von Reaktor plutonium (IANUS Institute fur kernphysik, Techniche Hochschule Darmstadt).

NUCLEAR POWER AND NON-PROLIFERATION: WHERE TO DRAW THE LINE

JESSICA TUCHMAN MATHEWS

ESTIMATING ENERGY NEEDS

The degree of proliferation risk from commercial use of nuclear energy is highly dependent on the amount of installed power. The greater the amount of material that must be safely handled, transported, and stored, and the greater the likelihood that heavy dependence on nuclear energy will lead to the use of plutonium fuel cycles, the greater the possibility that a significant quantity of critical material will be diverted to weapons use. The degree of dependence on nuclear power in turn depends most heavily on overall energy demand. Hence, estimating long-term proliferation risk from the nuclear-power sector requires a reliable estimation of total energy needs.

Long-term energy projections, however, are well-known to be a highly uncertain undertaking. In fact, only one characteristic is shared by the thousands of energy projections carried out in the 1970s and 1980s—the heyday of energy policy studies: All of them greatly exaggerated future demand.

Since analytic methodologies have changed very little since then, there is every reason to believe that current projections, particularly official government ones (which include virtually all of those relating to nuclear power), today suffer from the same flaw. Indeed, even the most recent projections for the Organisation for Economic Co-operation and Development (OECD) countries, the most studied and best understood energy economies, show the identical trend; a large overestimate of future demand that grows bigger the farther ahead one looks.

Understanding of future energy needs in the developing countries is considerably weaker than that of the mature energy economies. These countries have far less sunk cost in old energy technologies and hence much greater freedom to adopt new and more efficient technologies. They also generally have greater capital constraints, and they face environmental pressures—especially where growth is very rapid—that are both growing and changing. For these reasons, all energy projections, and especially those for developing countries, should be approached with a good deal of skepticism. The potential of improved energy efficiency—not conservation, but new technology—in both energy supply and end-use remains as unreflected in energy studies today as we now know it to have been twenty-five years ago.

This is particularly true for developing countries, where the efficiency of energy use (also known as energy intensity, its inverse, the amount of energy used per dollar of gross domestic product) is much lower than in the OECD countries, with much greater room for improvement at low cost. For example, average electricity losses in transmission and distribution are 50-100 percent higher in developing countries than in OECD countries. On average, investments in improving energy efficiency in developing countries yield energy savings of 20-25 percent, with economic payback periods of two years or less. Costs in this range are far lower than those of providing any new energy source.

THE NEED FOR NEW ENERGY INVESTMENT

Even if policy changes were to be made that would drive an unprecedented emphasis on improved efficiency, population increase, urbanization, and economic growth trends make clear that heavy investment in new energy supply will be needed as well. Today's energy growth rates are seven times higher in developing countries than in the OECD nations and will continue to rise much faster than in the industrialized countries. That said, however, it is highly unlikely that the very rapid energy growth projected for Asia, in particular, will be met, due to both financial and environmental constraints.

Most such projections (for example, by the International Atomic Energy Agency, the World Energy Council, and the World Bank) assume rates of investment in energy infrastructure that are two to four times today's levels—a total of $1.7-$4 trillion over the next two decades. By contrast, the World Bank today lends less than $4 billion per year for energy, while commercial bank lending for these projects has been declining. Though foreign direct investment is likely to rise, it too is subject to constraints and will not make up the difference. Just as in the past, assumed levels of future investment that are wildly out of kilter with present practice are simply unlikely to materialize.

In addition, every energy source—with the exception of improved energy efficiency—has substantial environmental drawbacks. Over the next twenty years, air quality, displacement of people, land shortages for agriculture, and greenhouse gas emissions are likely to be the primary environmental considerations in Asia and (with the possible exception of land shortages) worldwide. Governments' appreciation of the real costs of environmental degradation, rising public demand for environmental protection, and limits imposed by, for example, agricultural land losses, all suggest that environmental considerations will increasingly have impact on energy policies in the years ahead.

THE GROWTH OF ELECTRICITY DEMAND

Notwithstanding these constraints, energy use in Asia and elsewhere will grow substantially, and electricity demand will grow fastest. One recent analysis projects a tripling of electricity use, from 2,668 terawatt hours (TWh) in 1993 to 6,958 TWh in 2010 in the Asia-Pacific region.[1]

As has happened so often in the past, however, this analysis used official projections for nuclear power growth, averaging 6.6 percent/year, that the authors themselves do not believe. Unwilling either to jettison the official numbers, or to candidly state their incredulity, the authors merely comment that these projections "may be highly exaggerated," particularly in the case of Japan, Taiwan, and China. Seasoned energy analysts know how to interpret that veiled comment.

The eventual choices for the particular mix of sources will depend on a shifting balance of incentives and drawbacks. Greenhouse warming and air quality concerns may become a powerful spur to greater use of nuclear energy in the mid-term, that is, within the next two decades. The principal drawbacks will continue to be heavy investment costs and long construction leadtimes, high operating costs, political and technical difficulties associated with waste disposal (particularly in very population-dense countries), and public opinion on the use of nuclear energy and the dangers of nuclear proliferation.

All but the last of these are reasonably predictable and to some degree within the control of national governments. Two other "wild cards" that could substantially determine nuclear energy's future should also be noted. A serious nuclear power plant accident, a "second Chernobyl," either in the former Soviet Union, where current plant-safety conditions are known to be very poor, or anywhere else in the world, would severely affect prospects for new construction worldwide.

A less clearcut issue is that raised by the hugely negative public reaction to the French underground nuclear tests in the fall of 1995. Demonstrations and opposition from Auckland to Santiago were so intense and so much larger than even testing opponents had expected —and, one might add, so much larger than the actual risks of underground testing justify—that they raise the question of where public feelings on nuclear energy in general may be heading. The most one can say at this is point is that the evolution of public opinion is impossible to predict but foolish to ignore. Perhaps the most important unknown, however, is the possibility of proliferation through theft of highly enriched uranium (HEU) or plutonium from Russia. That country currently has at least 500 tons of excess, poorly guarded HEU—enough to make 40,000 nuclear weapons. HEU can be easily blended down to non –weapons-usable reactor fuel, but numerous problems stand in the way of that attractive solution, not the least of which is that so much material would flood an already soft world market for enriched uranium.

PLUTONIUM DIVERSION: THE TERRORIST DANGER

The risks of a plutonium diversion are even greater. Plutonium emits only alpha radiation and requires an extremely small amount for a critical mass. There are no known disposal options that are both environmentally and economically feasible. The combination yields an extremely severe proliferation threat in the coming years.

The plutonium being removed from weapons under U.S.–Russian arms control agreements may be reasonably well guarded by the Russian military. However, materials security at Russia's many civilian energy facilities is abysmal. Without a huge and very expensive effort to improve it, the likelihood of losses in the coming years is high. One serious nuclear terrorist incident, besides being tragic in itself, could well shut down new construction in the nuclear power industry around the world. It would certainly spell the end to further separation of plutonium from spent fuel, further raising the importance of an early demonstration in the United States or elsewhere of a technically reliable and politically acceptable nuclear waste disposal technology.

The absence of a major proliferation leak, particularly to criminal or terrorist groups, is essential to nuclear energy's long-term health. For this reason, as well as its clear lack of economic competitiveness (see Gilinsky chapter in this book), reprocessing and further accumulation of plutonium for use in civilian breeder reactors should be strongly avoided.

Notes

[1] Fereidun Fesharaki, Allen Clark, and Duangjai Intarapravich, eds., *Pacific Energy Outlook: Strategies and Policy Imperatives to 2010.* March, 1995. East-West Center, Honolulu, Hawaii.

NUCLEAR POWER AND NON-PROLIFERATION: WHERE TO DRAW THE LINE

ATSUYUKI SUZUKI

The differences between reactor-grade and weapon-grade nuclear materials have been discussed extensively. One major issue concerns the similarities and differences between reactor-grade and weapon-grade plutonium. All agree that reactor-grade plutonium could be used to make nuclear weapons and therefore should be subject to safeguard inspections. However, there is some disagreement over how easily reactor-grade plutonium could be used in weapons production.

FEASIBILITY OF USING REACTOR-GRADE PLUTONIUM IN WEAPONS PRODUCTION

American nuclear experts think that a special design is required if reactor-grade plutonium is to be used in a weapon, since the large number of neutrons released from the spontaneous nuclear fission of plutonium-240 leads to a high probability of pre-detonation. Such a special design is technically possible. Problems caused by radiation and heat from plutonium-238 or americium-241 created by the beta decay of plutonium-241 must also be considered, yet it seems that technical solutions to these problems could be devised.

In a 1976 telegram from Washington to U.S. embassies worldwide, sent after India had tested a plutonium device in 1974, the United States revealed for the first time an official judgment that reactor-grade plutonium could be used to make nuclear weapons. The most notable aspect of the telegram is its assertion that reactor-grade plutonium potentially could be used as a raw material for weapons by national governments, as distinct from its use by terrorist groups. Realistically, is such diversion at the national level likely to occur? It seems not. It would be much easier for a government to produce weapon-grade plutonium in a small facility or a clandestine plant rather than to use reactor-grade plutonium. North Korea is an obvious example of this logic. Although the plutonium which caused some problems in North Korea had been recovered from the spent fuel of a power reactor, it was considered to be weapon-grade plutonium because of its isotopic composition. Furthermore, it must be noted that using plutonium recovered as a

88

nuclear fuel after reprocessing spent fuel has no economic implications for countries that have extremely small nuclear power–generation capacities, as does North Korea, i.e., 50 MWe compared with more than 40,000 MWe in Japan.

My opinion is that the use of reactor-grade plutonium for nuclear weapons is theoretically possible, but so impractical that it is unlikely. This does not mean that I advocate excluding reactor-grade plutonium from safeguard inspections, or that I favor reducing efforts to prevent the diversion of this material to military applications. Enriched uranium is subject to a different level of safeguard inspection according to the extent of enrichment, and reactor-grade plutonium should be as well. I believe that the extent of inspection efforts is an important question for future consideration.

HANDLING AND DISPOSAL OF PLUTONIUM

Although it is unlikely that reactor-grade plutonium will be used to make nuclear weapons, plutonium of any grade is a hazardous substance, and an inability to account for this material can have huge social impact. Thus, physically protecting plutonium from terrorists and others when it is being handled is important. However, it should be noted that the purposes of so-called physical protection and of safeguard inspections are fundamentally different.

Many people have concerns about how nuclear materials from weapons dismantled in the process of disarmament are to be handled. In a 1994 report, the U.S. National Academy of Sciences estimated that about 100 tons of plutonium will be released during the next ten years in the United States and Russia as a result of dismantling nuclear weapons.[1] The report points out that these materials should be disposed of as early as possible for anti-proliferation reasons, and proposes the following two options: the first is to consume them in currently operating light-water reactors or the Canadian-type of heavy-water reactors; the second is "vitrification," followed by geological disposal, where plutonium would be mixed with high-level radioactive waste.

Regardless of which option is chosen, it is important to note that the United States and Russia ultimately must be responsible for how materials from their dismantled weapons are handled. If an international effort is made to dispose of plutonium from dismantled weapons, the United States and Russia must assure that the materials have been made irreversibly unfit for military use and that any potential for reproducing the material has been eliminated. Otherwise it may be difficult to gain the cooperation of third countries, such as Japan, that rigorously oppose any nuclear activities related to non-peaceful purposes.

It is unlikely that Russia will find disposal by vitrification to be an acceptable solution. In the United States as well, disposal after vitrification is problematical because several difficulties have been encountered in disposing of vitrified high-level radioactive waste at Yucca Mountain, Nevada, and the waste containing plutonium from military facilities at Carlsbad, New Mexico. Furthermore, countries such as the United Kingdom, France, and Japan—which emphasize recycling for most effective use of resources—may find that cooperating in disposal of a useful and valuable resource is inconsistent with their policies.

The alternative method, to consume plutonium fabricated as plutonium-and-uranium mixed oxide (MOX) fuels in nuclear reactors, is more likely to gain multilateral cooperation. However, the National Academy report makes the valid comment that developing or building new reactors specifically for this purpose is economically unjustifiable, since it seems likely that MOX fuels, manufactured with plutonium from dismantled weapons, can be completely consumed by operating existing reactors effectively.

CALCULATING PLUTONIUM CONSUMPTION

It is relevant to note that Japan has built the domestically developed prototype fast reactor called Monju and the prototype advanced thermal reactor called Fugen. Both were built for the purposes of research and development and are owned by the Power Reactor and Nuclear Fuel Development Corporation, a governmental research organization. Both were originally designed to use MOX fuels rather than uranium fuels.

I have attempted to calculate how much plutonium as MOX fuel could be consumed by these two reactors. Using current design and safety criteria and assuming that as much plutonium as possible should be consumed, I found that each reactor could consume about 1 ton of plutonium per year, or a total of 2 tons per year. If 100 tons of plutonium are to be freed up by weapons dismantling over the course of ten years in the United States and Russia, or 50 tons in each country, that makes an average of 5 tons per country per year. Japan would be making a significant contribution if it were to dispose of 2 tons of Russian plutonium each year.

There are also about fifty light-water reactors operating in Japan. Using recovered military plutonium in such reactors is technically possible, but since all are operated entirely by the private sector, it would be extremely difficult to gain the acceptance of local inhabitants and the general public for consuming foreign plutonium in these facilities even if the material were first made unfit for military use. Plutonium is intended to be used in these reactors strictly and only as part of the process of appropriately managing spent fuel. Thus Japanese utility companies have nothing to gain by substituting Russian plutonium for plutonium to be recycled in Japanese light-water reactors.

INEVITABILITY OF PROLIFERATION RISK

It may be possible to reduce the risk of nuclear proliferation, but not to eliminate it. In other words, we should make every effort to reduce the risk of proliferation, but we must at the same time recognize that the risk is inevitable.

Recognition of the inevitability of proliferation risk is important in a country such as Japan, which advances the use of nuclear power under the restriction that such technology be used only for peaceful purposes. Japanese tend to think that nuclear technology is developed and used only for peaceful purposes in their country and that this perception is accepted abroad, but they should always be aware that some people in other countries believe Japan will possess nuclear arms someday.

TRANSPARENCY AND DISCLOSURE

The best way to alleviate such concerns is for Japan to make its nuclear strategy more transparent. Especially when sensitive materials such as plutonium and enriched uranium are used in Japan, it is important that related information be disclosed so that methods and schedules for use of the materials, as well as existing conditions such as inventories and locations, can always be readily discerned.

Japan's plutonium inventory has been disclosed annually since 1993. In the cases of power-reactor facilities such as Monju and Fugen, as well as the reprocessing plant and MOX-fuel manufacturing facility at Tokai-mura, inventories and chemical forms for each facility and each process have been disclosed. Furthermore, information about inventories of Japanese plutonium stores at reprocessing plants in the United Kingdom and France also has been disclosed.

No other country discloses its current plutonium inventory in such detail. (The kilogram is the unit of quantity in these inventories.) Data disclosed by the United States are rough compared with the Japanese data; the United States reports only overall quantities in tons as distinct from the breakdown in Japanese inventories. The cumulative "hold-up" amount of plutonium that cannot be accounted for at the MOX-fuel manufacturing facility in Tokai-mura is about 70 kg—a problem to which the Japanese media have devoted considerable attention. Efforts to track down the missing material are now under way in collaboration with the International Atomic Energy Agency (IAEA), and the IAEA is confirming that material management data on plutonium at the facility are appropriate. Is it possible to acquire such fine-grained material management data on plutonium at U.S. military facilities? Probably not, considering the complexity and problems of the various radioactive wastes that contain plutonium and are stored at domestic U.S. military facilities.

Rather than quantitative accuracy, the most important issue in transparency is whether the content and operation of the facility are readily discernible. As long as human beings are involved in plant operation, it will be impossible to prove that there is absolutely no risk of nuclear proliferation. However, such concerns can be minimized by maintaining transparency in the operational and management status of the facility. At least the IAEA has no concerns over the risk of proliferation in connection with the MOX-fuel manufacturing facility at Tokai-mura.

COOPERATION IN EAST ASIA

These concepts of transparency may be applicable to international nuclear cooperation in East Asia. There are many countries in the region that are enthusiastic about developing nuclear power. China is a prime example. It is important that each country open its programs and actual status to other countries if the development of nuclear energy in East Asia is to proceed smoothly and the risk of nuclear proliferation simultaneously is to be minimized. Promoting an ASIATOM concept is a reasonable approach to achieving this state of affairs. Yet, East Asia is home to China, with its huge population, as well as to South and North Korea, which are in conflict—not to mention Russia's close presence. Under these circumstances, it may be difficult to create an effective forum without the participation of the United States.

Some may raise alarms over the potential for a double standard, arguing that if Japan can use plutonium, other countries must be able to do so as well. My opinion is that a double standard should not be adopted, and that each country should have the right to use plutonium after meeting certain requirements—transparency about projects and actual situations being the foremost. North Korea did not meet this requirement for transparency to the satisfaction of the United States and the IAEA.

The differences between military and peaceful-use facilities arise to no small extent from the transparency factor. Reprocessing plants are typical examples of this. Military reprocessing plants built in the past have caused serious environmental degradation in the United Kingdom and France as well as in the United States. However, the environmental safety of the reprocessing plant at La Hague, France, which is operated as a peaceful-use facility, is so much better than that of old military facilities that they are beyond comparison. As opposed to military facilities, peaceful-use facilities cannot be accepted by local inhabitants or the general public if they do not offer sufficient guarantees for environmental safety.

Thorough transparency in plant-operation status is required to gain public acceptance; consequently, the transparency factor creates great motivation to improve the environmental safety of a facility. Transparency must be viewed not only as an aid in reducing the risk of nuclear proliferation, but even more as a top-priority requirement for the future development and use of nuclear energy.

Note

[1] *The Management and Disposition of Excess Weapons Plutonium* (U.S. National Academy Press, Washington, 1994), p. 5.

ASIATOM: HOW SOON, WHAT ROLE, AND WHO SHOULD PARTICIPATE?

WILLIAM J. DIRCKS

The projected growth of nuclear power, along with accompanying growth in fuel-cycle facilities in Asia, has led a number of writers to discuss the feasibility of establishing an Asian regional compact similar to the Europe-based European Atomic Energy Community (EURATOM) to foster cooperation in nuclear operations, develop regional standards for safe operations, provide an additional level of safeguards beyond the IAEA regime, and establish a regional policy on nuclear exports.

There are significant differences, however, between the conditions in Europe in the 1960s, when EURATOM was founded, and those in Asia in the 1990s. These differences must be dealt with before an ASIATOM can replicate the transparency and confidence levels that exist in the European nuclear community.

ASIA: MAJOR CENTER OF NUCLEAR GROWTH

China, Japan, Korea, and Taiwan already have large numbers of nuclear plants in operation and have announced plans for major additional expansions. All four countries already have the capacity to meet their own internal demand and the ability to export nuclear plants and fuels.

Indonesia and Thailand have also developed plans for nuclear power plants and have already started site selection. If India and Pakistan are included in this discussion, then the Asian region can readily be described as the most dominant center of world activity in nuclear power.

In addition to nuclear plants, a network of supporting nuclear fuel-cycle support activities is already in place. The Japanese nuclear fuel cycle is the most discussed because of the completeness of the cycle encompassing enrichment facilities at the front end and a highly developed network of facilities at the back end of the cycle, including reprocessing, recycling, and fuel-fabrication facilities.

Fuel-cycle industrial development is also proceeding rapidly in other Asian nations. Beginning in the early days of its military program, China constructed a self-contained nuclear fuel cycle. These facilities are now under the management of the China National Nuclear Corporation (CNNC), which has declared its intention to offer fuel-cycle services over a full range of commercial export markets. Included

94

in this offer would be the output of its gaseous diffusion plant and its new centrifuge plant. From the outset of its commercial nuclear power program, China has made clear its intention to reprocess spent fuel and recycle MOX fuel in its light-water and breeder reactors.

China has also made clear its intentions to be an active competitor in the international nuclear power facilities marketplace offering both completed nuclear plants and a full range of fuels services. China sees this market as a large potential source of hard currency.

South Korea's per capita electric usage is only one-half of Japan's (which is half of U.S. usage). Residential use is 20 percent of consumption, and over 60 percent is industrial. South Korea's total demand growth has regularly exceeded 10 percent a year, but with drastic conservation efforts, South Korea hopes to bring the growth rate down to 6.5 percent between now and 2005. Because Korea must import all its fuels, it has declared a deliberate policy of nuclear-power construction to bring one new plant on line each year. Baseload reactors now generate 50 percent of South Korea's electric power.

South Korea does not own enrichment or reprocessing facilities and relies on Europe and the United States for its fuel. In the 1970s, it attempted to purchase a reprocessing plant but was blocked by the United States. Twice since then, it has attempted to secure reprocessing-related technology but did not succeed. Although South Korea and North Korea signed an agreement not to reprocess on the Korean peninsula, there is concern that a unified Korea would try again to develop a self-contained fuel cycle to service the large and growing number of nuclear-power facilities.

Other Asian nations are firmly in the nuclear camp or making firm plans to get there. Taiwan has 35 percent of its electricity generated by nuclear-power plants and plans to add at least six more units by the year 2005. Its electric reserve margins are down to 5 percent and brownouts are common events. Here, too, the nuclear program plans are based on the need for security of supply.

Indonesia is just in the beginning phase of site selection for a nuclear plant. It feels it needs nuclear power for energy security. To assure fuel supply security and deal with waste, Indonesia plans to call for construction of its own reprocessing capability.

NEED FOR LESS NUCLEAR-POWER SELF-RELIANCE AND MORE REGIONAL COOPERATION

Major expansion of nuclear power along the lines of these projections will overload the technical capabilities and control institutions that currently exist in Asian countries. These countries have diverse backgrounds and varying attitudes on issues such as trade-offs between economic development and safety and non-proliferation objectives. Moving ahead with relatively small-scale national efforts could have a serious impact not only on public health and international security but also on the viability of national nuclear programs themselves.

In the area of safety, for example, Japan has the most to gain by working toward an effort to set high performance standards in neighboring Asian countries. The Japanese nuclear program's safety record is among the world's best. This history of rigorous adherence to high safety standards is one of the major reasons for continued Japanese public acceptance of nuclear power.

However, strong public support of the Japanese program is also linked to the performance of nuclear plants in other Asian countries. An accident in any one of these countries could conceivably affect Japanese public health, and would most certainly have a major impact on continued Japanese public acceptance of nuclear power.

All countries within the region would benefit from safety improvements in plants in the region, but those countries with established nuclear programs would benefit most. Indeed, even Europe and the United States have a stake in achieving this goal. Based on the lesson of Chernobyl and Three Mile Island, public perceptions of the safety of nuclear power are the foundations for any national nuclear program.

Safe and reliable operation of nuclear facilities would in itself be an important reason for the formation of a regional grouping of governments in Asia, but the creation of an effective means to control the product and fuels from nuclear fuel-cycle facilities would be even more beneficial. The development of small-scale enrichment and reprocessing facilities in individual Asian states handling large amounts of sensitive material would represent serious challenges to existing non-proliferation regimes.

EURATOM from its beginnings had two principal objectives: assurance of fuel supplies and assurance that the material would not be diverted to unintended purposes. The rationale for any Asian regional nuclear compact would necessarily encompass these two objectives. EURATOM has constructed a deep, extensive, and intrusive system of controls on plants and materials that include both a large, highly trained and expert staff of inspectors and the use of high-tech in plant monitoring systems. In addition, EURATOM has developed a common European set of standards dealing with export controls.

There must be a clear understanding that IAEA and NPT safeguards still apply under a regional program. Some Asian industrial operators have felt that the IAEA's safeguards system is too intrusive and costly, and that inspectors from an ASIATOM organization staffed by

Asian citizens would be more understanding of Asian industrial prac-
tices. However, regional systems are an extra layer of safeguards and not
a substitute for IAEA.

In addition to the safety, safeguards, and exportcontrol functions
of EURATOM, some Asian writers have discussed regional nuclear fuel-
cycle centers. This was an important concept both in the 1980
International Nuclear Fuel Cycle Evaluation (INFCE) Report and in the
Department of Energy's NASAP (Non-Proliferation Alternative
Systems Assessment Program) Report of 1979. In place of nationally
owned and nationally operated reprocessing and enrichment plants, the
goal would be to have one or two large plants to service the Asian
market.

The regional Fuel-Cycle Center as envisioned in the INFCE
Report could be owned by a regional state or could be operated under
broader multinational supervision and management. National needs
would have to be treated equitably, and all states would have a right to
use the facility. The INFCE concept never came to fruition for many
reasons relating to the issue of ownership rights and access rights to the
products from the plant, such as the MOX fuel.

A REGIONAL NUCLEAR COMPACT FOR ASIA:
WHAT ARE ITS PROSPECTS?

At first reading, there would appear to be benefits to moving toward
the establishment of an Asian regional nuclear organization. Asian
states in the organization could work out a regional set of safety standards and develop systems of monitoring adhering to those standards.
The organization could develop a comprehensive set of safeguards and
verification procedures, and it could develop the necessary advanced
technology required for fuel-cycle material control and security systems.
Even though the complexities loom large, it could perhaps work toward
regionally owned and managed fuel-cycle centers. Finally, like
EURATOM, it could develop a binding set of export-control policies. In
short, it could bring an added dimension of transparency and some
degree of regulatory oversight to the nationally based nuclear fuel cycles
being developed in Asia.

However, there are some obstacles that would have to be overcome before such an organization could even begin to deal with confronting rapidly developing nuclear deployment in Asia. The size of
membership is important, as is the need to assure some uniformity in
terms of economic strength, political systems that are open and transparent, and, paradoxically, some degree of diversity as to views of
nuclear-power risks and benefits. These are present in the EURATOM

agency, and they bring in a built-in stabilizing system. An organization dominated by two economic giants—China and Japan—whose energy programs are tied so tightly to heavy investments in developing a nuclear fuel cycle, may have difficulties in securing the open system of checks and balances that exists in Europe or even in smaller regional compacts such as the Argentine-Brazil Regional Organization. Yet without China, the organization loses a major reason for its existence.

The key to the creation of the organization is China. It represents the area of greatest nuclear growth potential and has become active in the international nuclear marketplace. China, however, has traditionally resisted joining any regional or alignment blocs. It has always regarded itself as being equal to any regional grouping because of its size and population. It also is a nuclear-weapon state and may fear losing some of the privileges attached to that status. China would also resist the placement of any restrictions on itself in the export field. China is developing a large industrial capacity in the nuclear field that will soon overwhelm the capabilities of its internal market to absorb its output. China may then become even more willing than it has been in the past to cut corners in selling to high-risk countries. These obstacles are considerable, yet an Asian regional nuclear organization without China loses much of its relevance. A possible way to get China in and broaden the mix of membership would be to include other Pacific Rim states such as Australia, Canada, and even the United States, creating not ASIATOM but a Pacific Atomic Energy Community (PACATOM).

ASIATOM OR PACATOM?

Australia, because of its ties to Asia as well as its large uranium deposits, could easily qualify for membership in a cooperative regional nuclear organization. With its strong non-proliferation credentials, Australia would indeed strengthen the balance of the organization. But if Australia were included, why not Canada? The same rationale supporting Australia's membership in the organization would support Canada's. Canada is a developed nuclear-power country with an impeccable safety and non-proliferation record.

The tricky issue then is the question of the United States. U.S. interests would be served by inclusion in a PACATOM and, more to the point, the interests of other members of the compact would be served equally well. U.S. participation could also serve as an added inducement for China to join. Both are nuclear-weapon states and both are large continental nations. Some major problems in expanding the ASIATOM to a PACATOM would have to be faced, but the benefits of the larger balanced membership might be well worth the costs.

Still other issues would have to be addressed if efforts are made to create either an ASIATOM or a PACATOM. For example: What would be the role of North Korea? How would India and Pakistan relate to the new organization? Could Taiwan join, and how would China react?

SLOW START NEEDED TO PROVE THE USEFULNESS OF A PACATOM OR ASIATOM

Initially, the effort to create a new organization should start with limited objectives. It might, for example, develop a technical-exchange and support program on safety performance, a clearinghouse mechanism on fuel supply, and a regionally based plutonium-management regime. Agreement with the IAEA on increasing the efficiency and effectiveness of a regional safeguards system would be another example of an initial step showing the usefulness of the organization.

At each step, the building of confidence among member states could lead to taking on the more difficult tasks, such as developing concepts for export controls and regional fuel-cycle management.

Regionally based nuclear organization systems are being used more frequently. PACATOM (or ASIATOM) would not have to be a replica of EURATOM but could take on its own form in order to deal with the problems of a developed nuclear industry in Asia.

ASIATOM: HOW SOON, WHAT ROLE, AND WHO SHOULD PARTICIPATE?

MAKOTO ISHII

J apan's nuclear energy policy is undergoing historic change as what was once purely domestic policy becomes foreign policy. Until now, the core objective of the country's nuclear energy policy has been to develop domestic nuclear power generation. Technologies for resource exploration, power reactor, enrichment, and reprocessing have been developed for the purpose of structuring a domestic nuclear fuel cycle. There have been no exports related to nuclear power generation.

A 1995 report of the Energy Study Group of the Ministry of International Trade and Industry (MITI) stated that Japan will enhance its export of products related to nuclear energy while considering the safety of Asia's developing nuclear power. The Atomic Energy Commission has begun to discuss policies concerning nuclear energy in Asia. Now is an appropriate time to discuss the concept of an Asian Atomic Energy Community (ASIATOM) and how it should be implemented.

A strictly defined ASIATOM organization should not be established in undue haste. Instead, it would be reasonable to establish the constituent elements, one by one, as each becomes feasible, while keeping an eye on the likelihood of future developments, and to complete the structure at a later date, perhaps by the year 2020. Since nuclear energy development entails a long lead-time, planning should start promptly.

Following are the proposed constituent elements of ASIATOM:

- A regional safeguards system,
- A regional nuclear fuel cycle,
- A nuclear-power safety system, and
- An organization for cooperation on research and development.

REGIONAL SAFEGUARDS SYSTEM

A nuclear non-proliferation system should be established in anticipation of the expanded use of atomic energy in East Asia. ASIATOM could provide the base for a regional system of safeguards which would be an effective means to this end. There are still deep-rooted fears in East Asia that Japan may take up nuclear arms and that nuclear weapons may be developed on the Korean Peninsula. A regional safeguards system could relieve such doubts, create mutual reliance, and consequently prevent nuclear temptations in the region.

Such a system—whether it consisted of establishing a nuclear-free zone, disarmament, or arms-control schemes—would be an important factor in achieving regional security. Plans could proceed in the following three phases:

> *First phase:* Relevant countries in the region prepare and standardize nuclear-material accountancy systems for controlling nuclear substances.
>
> *Second phase:* All countries in the region exchange data on their nuclear-material accountancy systems and conduct mutual inspections.
>
> *Third phase:* Nuclear-material accountancy systems in the region are integrated, and a European Atomic Energy Community (EURATOM)–type of organization is established.

All of East Asia, including countries that have or plan to have nuclear power generation plants or research reactors, should participate in the system.

REGIONAL NUCLEAR FUEL CYCLE

Establishment of a nuclear fuel cycle—which includes enrichment, reconversion, and fuel manufacturing and reprocessing—is necessary in order to expand nuclear power generation in a stable manner. It is reasonable to create a multilateral nuclear fuel cycle in East Asia.

Construction of enrichment and reprocessing facilities by Japan and West Germany was approved under the standards of the International Nuclear Fuel Cycle Evaluation (INFCE), with its concept of gradual evolution to justify building certain facilities in a country after a particular scale of nuclear power generation has been achieved. South Korea and Taiwan are close to becoming qualified to build such facilities according to this concept. A plan for the nuclear fuel cycle is now being implemented in China. It is expected that several countries in East Asia will require the use of full-scale enrichment and fuel manufacturing and reprocessing facilities early in the 21st century, and that their needs will continue to expand for a long time.

If these operations are conducted as a multilateral project, participating countries could economize on high development costs and at the same time be assured of access to needed services. From the standpoint of nuclear non-proliferation, a smaller number of such facilities is better. The transparency of the relevant processes will improve if international systems for storing plutonium and managing nuclear spent fuel are introduced.

The extent to which nuclear power generation has been or will be developed in East Asia differs from country to country. Recycling may not be economically attractive to those countries which have recently introduced nuclear power generation. However, viewed from a long-term perspective, the nuclear fuel cycle is indispensable for all countries. Therefore, realistic concepts of a regional nuclear fuel-cycle project will need to be flexible, first envisioning an overall scheme for the nuclear fuel cycle in East Asia, and then making it possible for countries to begin participating in relevant aspects of the project as their needs arise.

Various proposals have been made for the form of such a project: a multilateral project; a single-country project with the participation of multiple partners; and an international public fuel corporation. The overall concept should be discussed as soon as possible. Hiroshi Murata, Vice President of the Japan Atomic Industrial Forum, has proposed a plan that includes constructing enrichment facilities in Australia with Japanese technology, fuel manufacturing facilities in South Korea and Indonesia, and reprocessing and waste disposal facilities in China.

MULTILATERAL FRAMEWORK FOR A
NUCLEAR-POWER SAFETY SYSTEM

The issue of establishing a safety assurance system has become urgent for Asian countries that are expanding or introducing nuclear power generation. The report compiled by the MITI energy study group proposes establishing a multilateral framework to cope with new developments. The countries to be involved are those on the Pacific Rim that are now operating nuclear power plants or are planning to do so. The topics to be discussed include:

- Raising safety awareness in participating countries as well as across the region;

- Preparing for safety agreements between participating countries and across the region; a regional emergency contact system in case of an accident;

- Mutual assistance systems;

- Regional preparations on compensation for damage suffered by a third country caused by a nuclear energy accident or another event; and

- Measures to control or dispose of radioactive waste and nuclear spent fuel.

The Science and Technology Agency is planning to establish an international safety technology center for the region within the Japan

Atomic Energy Research Institute. The center will provide countries in the region with a system to predict how radioactive substances will diffuse if an accident occurs and will supply data from relevant safety studies and past accidents.

A multilateral framework for safety measures will deepen mutual dependence and reliance among countries in the region. It will also serve to increase public acceptance of nuclear energy. Multilateral discussions on the formation of such a framework should start soon.

AN ASIAN ORGANIZATION FOR COOPERATION ON NUCLEAR RESEARCH AND DEVELOPMENT

The three elements of this organization would be:

■ Establish ASIATOM international research institute for nuclear energy: a research institute for basic and applied studies is established in Japan to support participating countries. Branches are established locally. The regional level of technology improves and mutual dependence is promoted.

■ Joint fastbreeder reactor (FBR) development project; in anticipation of the use of plutonium in the future, FBR development activities are promoted centering on Japan, South Korea, and China.

■ Joint studies are conducted on issues common to East Asian countries.

III.

THE
FUTURE
OF
NUCLEAR
FORCES

WORKING GROUP III

Co-Chairmen
Steven E. Miller and Ryukichi Imai

John E. Endicott
Takehiko Kamo
Robert S. McNamara
Satoshi Morimoto

THE FUTURE OF NUCLEAR FORCES

REPORT OF WORKING GROUP III

The discussions of the working group focused on START II, ballistic missile defenses, the U.S. nuclear posture, conditionality and the NPT, prospects for a nuclear-free zone in Northeast Asia, the possibility of an East Asian nuclear fuel-cycle center, and IAEA safeguards in relation to the region.

START II

The uncertain future of START II is a matter of great concern. The failure of the Russian Duma to ratify the treaty would mean collapse of the main edifice of post–Cold War nuclear arms control, and a setback in efforts to achieve the further reduction of the world's nuclear weapons.

There is opposition in the Duma, and it is unlikely to ratify the treaty. One factor underlying this opposition is discussion in the West of the possible expansion of NATO eastward with the possible deployment of U.S. nuclear weapons. Another is the fact that the conventional forces in Russia are melting away, without new conscripts, new weapons, fuel, pilots, and even electricity. It is possible that under such circumstances, Russia may want to return to the days of decisive nuclear forces. Being a nuclear superpower may seem very important to Russia to maintain its prestige.

START II was not necessarily a well thought out scheme. President Yeltsin agreed to this treaty in haste in the aftermath of the dissolution of the Soviet Union. He seemed to have regretted it later, but the Bush Administration pressured Russia to sign in January 1993. START II is unfavorable to Russia, in that the United States can rely on SLBMs, in which it has a technical advantage, while Russia had to reduce mobile land-based ICBMs, in which its technical advantage lies. In reality, SLBMs and land-mobile ICBMs have almost equivalent nuclear deterrence capabilities. In addition, the agreed-upon 3,000/3,500 level is more expensive for Russia to maintain. It would have been better if the two countries had agreed to a lower level balance —which in any event would not have been very different in real terms, in view of the nature of nuclear deterrence (which does not depend on exact numerical equality). START treaties are binding on numbers of delivery vehicles and their platforms while warhead dismantling is a corollary. Thus, a lower level of balance could have been agreed upon in spite of limitations of warhead dismantling capabilities.

BALLISTIC MISSILE DEFENSES

American efforts to promote ballistic missile defenses (BMD) could widen the gap between Washington and Moscow on nuclear arms control. For one thing, BMD may be a violation of the Anti Ballistic Missile (ABM) Treaty. Moreover, if Russia is allowed to have missile defenses, some in the U.S. Congress may argue that this is destabilizing (as many argued in the ABM debate) and therefore oppose a START II level of nuclear forces.

Nuclear-material control in Russia is almost non-existent in a society no longer confined to closed cities and governed by internal passports. Good book-keeping procedures are conspicuously lacking. The consequences of this situation could become very serious if such nuclear material escapes into the black markets of the world. The time to act is now. But the Russian government is not interested or cooperative, and U.S. Congressional support for the Nunn-Lugar program of assistance to Russian denuclearization efforts is declining. None of the other Western governments has shown interest in this problem. In fact, Russia's unwillingness to comply with its commitments under the Conventional Forces in Europe (CFE) arrangements due to the Chechen insurgency and other concerns is reinforcing U.S. Congressional reluctance to continue funding denuclearization programs. A high level of transparency is desirable in the implementation of existing nuclear arms control agreements and of plans for cooperative efforts in dismantling nuclear weapons. But the reality is a trend away from such transparency at the expense of mutual confidence and trust.

THE U.S. NUCLEAR POSTURE

The 1994 U.S. Nuclear Posture Review failed to produce a convincing new post–Cold War nuclear doctrine and/or strategy that can logically lead to the further reduction of nuclear warheads going beyond START II. Although the Posture Review did not clearly spell out the U.S. position on the first use of nuclear weapons, it appears that the United States still maintains the "first use" option. The Posture Review goes hand in hand with the Pentagon's earlier "Bottom-Up Review"—with its assumption of two simultaneous wars on the scale of the Gulf War. It did not clarify the targeting and command and control concepts necessary to implement the 3,000/3,500 level of nuclear weapons envisaged in START II. Thus, it failed to set the stage for START III or for additional steps to reduce further the world's level of nuclear forces. It would appear that U.S. military leaders in both the conventional and nuclear fields are interested in preserving vested interests and are seeking to justify the continuation of the main lines of the status quo.

CONDITIONALITY AND THE NPT

The extension of the Nuclear Non-Proliferation Treaty (NPT) without firm conditionality (i.e., steps by the existing nuclear weapon states to reduce their own nuclear arsenals) may foreshadow future trouble. France and China may react to the absence of such conditionality by seeking to upgrade and modernize their submarine-launched ballistic missile forces, which could place the projected Comprehensive Test Ban Treaty in jeopardy.

Japan did not act very wisely in reacting to Chinese nuclear testing in 1995 with a cut in development assistance to China. Japan could have weighed the impact of this action on the chances for persuading China to join with the United States and Russia in reducing nuclear weapons to lower levels. After all, Japan has lived with numerous Chinese tests and weapons deployments in the past. There is a danger that China may be developing the mentality that it will face 3,000/3,500 warheads each in the hands of United States and Russia and must expand its own forces in response.

A NUCLEAR-FREE ZONE

A nuclear-free zone in East Asia involving portions of U.S., Chinese, and Russian territories is a worthwhile goal to explore as a means of forestalling a Chinese expansion of its nuclear-weapons program.

AN EAST ASIAN NUCLEAR FUEL-CYCLE CENTER?

Energy demand in East Asia is bound to increase very quickly along with rapid economic growth and population increases. This may lead to greater use of coal (and thus of acid rain) or increased levels of nuclear power generation. The option may be forced upon China very soon, and Japan is worried about the level of safety control in China's nuclear industry. The rapid expansion of nuclear energy in China, South Korea, Taiwan, Indonesia, and other ASEAN member states is conceivable. It therefore becomes important to consider the establishment of an East Asian nuclear fuel-cycle center or centers with sufficient international supervision to assure safety and to prevent the diversion of nuclear material for military purposes. It was argued that if an NPT-type inequality is to be accepted into the indefinite future, it may be possible and necessary—especially in the future handling of plutonium as nuclear fuel—to make distinctions between likely proliferation states and states firmly committed to non-proliferation.

IAEA SAFEGUARDS

An increase in nuclear power generation and thus an increase in nuclear fuel and plutonium throughout the world (in addition to U.S./Russian weapons plutonium) would mean that the current IAEA safeguards based on material accountancy may not be adequate. It may be useful to consider the possibilities of a new international safeguards institution and/or new arrangements, involving remote-sensing and other pertinent technologies, thus expanding "national technical means" verification (e.g., by U.S. satellites) into nuclear proliferation, and even environmental control.

THE NEED FOR A NUCLEAR POLICY DEBATE

The public indifference to and ignorance of nuclear issues in both the United States and Japan was noted with regret. Many policies that seem ill-suited to the age survive not because the public supports them but because the public is unaware of them. It was suggested that there is a need for vigorous and visible public debate in both countries on such subjects as the desirability of and requirements for minimum deterrence, the extent to which large-scale revisions of the nuclear posture should be impeded by concerns about hedging against a resurgent Russian threat, and the morality of the current nuclear posture and strategy. Better nuclear policy would derive from such a debate, not least because current policies would not withstand careful public scrutiny.

NEXT STEPS IN ARMS CONTROL:
HOW FAR, HOW FAST?

ROBERT S. McNAMARA

THE RISK OF DESTRUCTION

Today there are roughly 40,000-50,000 nuclear warheads in the world, with a total destructive power more than one million times greater than that of the bomb that flattened Hiroshima. Assuming the reductions called for by START I are achieved, the total weapons inventory will be reduced to approximately 20,000. Presidents Bush and Yeltsin agreed to further reductions that would leave the five declared nuclear powers (the United States, Russia, France, the United Kingdom, and China) with a total of about 10,000 warheads in 2003. It was a highly desirable move, but even if the U.S. Senate and the Russian Parliament ratify the agreement—and that is not at all certain—the risk of destruction of societies across the globe, while somewhat reduced, is far from eliminated. I doubt a survivor—if there were one—could perceive much difference between a world in which only 10,000 nuclear warheads had been exploded or 40,000. Can we not go further? Surely the answer must be *yes*.

The end of the Cold War, along with the growing understanding of the lack of utility of nuclear weapons and the high risk associated with their continued existence, points to both the opportunity and the urgency with which the five declared nuclear powers should re-examine their long-term nuclear force objectives. We should begin with a broad public debate over three alternative nuclear strategies, which I will outline. I believe such a debate would support the conclusion that, insofar as *achievable*, we should move back to a non-nuclear world.

In support of my position, I make the following three points:

1. The experience of the Cuban missile crisis in 1962 and, in particular, what has been learned about it recently, makes it clear that as long as we and other great powers possess large inventories of nuclear weapons, we will face the risk of their use.

2. That risk is no longer, if it ever was, justifiable on military grounds.

3. In recent years, there has been a dramatic change in the thinking of leading Western security experts about the military utility of

nuclear weapons. More and more of them, although certainly not yet a majority, are expressing views similar to those I have stated.

First, the Cuban missile crisis: It is now widely recognized that the actions of the Soviet Union, Cuba, and the United States in October 1962 brought the three nations to the verge of war. But what was not known then, and is not widely recognized today, was how close the world came to the brink of nuclear disaster. Neither the Soviet Union, nor Cuba or the United States intended by its actions to create such risks.

In 1962, during the crisis, some of us, particularly President Kennedy and I, believed the United States faced great dangers. That judgment was confirmed in two meetings that brought together many of those who had been involved in the crisis, one in Havana in January 1992, and one in Moscow in January 1993. The Havana meeting, in particular, made clear that both of us—and certainly others—had seriously underestimated those dangers. While in Havana, we were told by the former Warsaw Pact Chief of Staff, General Anatoly Gribkov, that, in 1962, Soviet forces in Cuba possessed not only nuclear warheads for the intermediate-range missiles, but nuclear bombs and tactical nuclear warheads as well. The tactical warheads were to be used against U.S. invasion forces. At the time, as I mentioned, the U.S. Central Intelligence Agency was reporting no warheads on the island. But in November 1992, we learned just how great the danger had been. An article appeared in the Russian press which stated that, at the height of the missile crisis, Soviet forces on Cuba possessed a total of 162 nuclear warheads, including at least 90 tactical warheads. Moreover, it was reported that, on October 26, 1962, a moment of great tension, warheads were moved from their storage sites to positions closer to their delivery vehicles in anticipation of a U.S. invasion.[1] The next day, Soviet Defense Minister Malinovsky received a cable from General Pliyev, the Soviet commander in Cuba, informing him of this action. Malinovsky sent it to Nikita Khrushchev. Khrushchev returned it to Malinovsky with "Approved" scrawled across the document. Clearly, the risk was high that, in the face of a U.S. attack, the Soviet forces in Cuba would have decided to use their nuclear weapons rather than lose them.[2]

We need not speculate about what would have happened in that event. We can predict the results with certainty. Although a U.S. invasion force would not have been equipped with tactical nuclear warheads —the President and I had specifically prohibited that—no one should believe that, had American troops been attacked with nuclear weapons, the United States would have refrained from a nuclear response. And where would it have ended? In utter disaster.

HUMAN FALLIBILITY AND NUCLEAR WEAPONS

The point I wish to emphasize is that human beings are fallible. We all make mistakes. In our daily lives, mistakes are costly, but we try to learn from them. In conventional war, they cost lives, sometimes thousands of lives. But if mistakes were to affect decisions relating to the use of nuclear forces, they would result in the destruction of nations. I believe, therefore, it can be predicted with confidence that the indefinite combination of human fallibility and nuclear weapons carries a high risk of a potential catastrophe.

Is there a military justification for continuing to accept that risk? The answer is no. In "Nuclear Weapons After the Cold War"[3] Carl Kaysen, George W. Rathjens, and I pointed out that proponents of nuclear weapons "have produced only one plausible scenario for their use: a situation where there is no prospect of retaliation, either against a non-nuclear state or against one so weakly armed as to permit the user to have full confidence in his nuclear forces' capability to achieve a totally disarming first strike." We added that "even such circumstances have not, in fact, provided a sufficient basis for the use of nuclear weapons in war. For example, although American forces were in desperate straits twice during the Korean War—first immediately following the North Korean attack in 1950 and then when the Chinese crossed the Yalu—the United States did not use nuclear weapons. At that time, North Korea and China had no nuclear capability and the Soviet Union only a negligible one."

The argument which Kaysen, Rathjens, and I made leads to the conclusion that the military utility of nuclear weapons is limited to deterring one's opponent from their use. Therefore, if our opponent has no nuclear weapons, there is no need for us to possess them.

Partly because of the increased understanding of how close we came to disaster during the Cuban missile crisis, but also because of a growing recognition of the lack of military utility of the weapons, there has been a revolutionary change in thinking about the role of nuclear forces. Much of this change has occurred in the past three years. Many military leaders—including, for example, two former Chairmen of the Joint Chiefs of Staff, a former Supreme Commander of Allied Forces in Europe, and a senior U.S. Air Force officer recently on active duty—are now prepared to go far beyond the Bush-Yeltsin agreement. Some go so far as to state, as I have, that the long-term objective should be a return, insofar as practical, to a non-nuclear world. These views have been reflected in three reports and numerous unclassified, but not widely disseminated, statements.

A REVOLUTIONARY CHANGE IN THINKING

The three reports have all been published since 1990:

1. In 1991, a committee of the U.S. National Academy of Sciences, in a report signed by retired Joint Chiefs of Staff Chairman General David C. Jones, stated: "nuclear weapons should serve no purpose beyond the deterrence of . . . nuclear attack by others." The committee believed U.S. and Russian nuclear forces could be reduced to 1,000-2,000 warheads.[4]

2. The Spring 1993 issue of Foreign Affairs carried an article co-authored by another retired Chairman of the Joint Chiefs of Staff, Admiral William J. Crowe, Jr., which concluded that by the year 2000, the United States and Russia could reduce strategic nuclear forces to 1,000-1,500 warheads each. The article was later expanded into a book which added: "Nor is 1,000-1,500 the lowest level obtainable by the early 21st Century."[5]

3. In August 1993, General Andrew J. Goodpaster, former Supreme Allied Commander of NATO Forces in Europe, published a report in which he said the five existing nuclear powers should be able to reduce nuclear weapons stockpiles to "no more than 200 each" and "the ultimate would be a 'zero level'" [emphasis in original].[6]

These three reports should not come as surprises. For nearly twenty years, more and more Western military and civilian security experts have expressed doubts about the military utility of nuclear weapons. For example:

■ By 1982, five of the seven retired Chiefs of the British Defense Staff had expressed their belief that initiating the use of nuclear weapons, in accordance with NATO policy, would lead to disaster. Lord Louis Mountbatten, Chief of Staff from 1959-65, said a few months before he was murdered in 1979: "As a military man I can see no use for any nuclear weapons." And Field Marshal Lord Carver, Chief of Staff from 1973-76, wrote in 1982 that he was totally opposed to NATO ever initiating the use of nuclear weapons.[7]

■ Admiral Noel Gaylor, former Commander-in-Chief of U.S. Air, Ground, and Sea forces in the Pacific, remarked in 1971: "There is no sensible military use of any of our nuclear forces. The only reasonable use is to deter our opponents from using his nuclear forces."[8]

■ Melvin Laird, President Nixon's first Secretary of Defense, was reported in The Washington Post of April 12, 1982, as saying: "A worldwide zero nuclear option with adequate verification should now be our goal. . . . These weapons . . . are useless for m purposes."[9]

- And in July 1994, General Charles A. Horner, then chief of the U.S. Space Command, stated: "The nuclear weapon is obsolete. I want to get rid of them all."[10]

In the early 1960s, I had reached conclusions similar to those cited above. In long private conversations, first with President Kennedy and then with President Johnson, I had recommended, without qualification, that they never initiate, under any circumstances, the use of nuclear weapons. I believe they accepted my recommendations.[11] But neither they nor I could discuss our position publicly because it was contrary to established NATO policy.

Today, given the totally contradictory views of supporters and opponents regarding the role of nuclear weapons, but with the recognition by all that initiation of the use of such weapons against a nuclear-equipped opponent would lead to disaster, should we not begin immediately to debate the merits of alternative long-term objectives for the five declared nuclear powers?

We could choose from three options:

1. A continuation of the present strategy of "extended deterrence," the strategy recently reconfirmed by the Administration.[12] This would mean limiting the United States and Russia to approximately 3,500 strategic warheads each, the figure agreed upon by Presidents Bush and Yelstin.[13]

2. A minimum deterrent force, as recommended by the U.S. National Academy of Sciences committee, and supported by General Jones and Admiral Crowe, with the two major nuclear powers retaining no more than 1,000-2,000 warheads each.

3. As General Goodpaster and I strongly advocate, a return by all five nuclear powers, insofar as practicable,[14] to a non-nuclear world.[15]

Notes

[1] General Gribkov elaborated on these points at a meeting at the Wilson Center that I attended in Washington, D.C., on April 5, 1994.

[2] See Anatoly Dokochaev, "Afterward to Sensational 100 Day Nuclear Cruise," *Krasnaya Zvezda,* November 6, 1992, p. 2; and V. Badurkin interview with Dimitri Volkogonov in "Operation Anadyr," *Trud,* October 27, 1992, p.3.

[3] See *Foreign Affairs,* Fall 1991, p. 95.

115

[4] *The Future of the U.S.–Soviet Nuclear Relationship* (Washington, D.C.: National Academy of Sciences, 1991), p. 3.

[5] McGeorge Bundy, William J. Crowe, Jr., and Sidney O. Drell, *Reducing Nuclear Danger: The Road Away from the Brink* (New York: Council on Foreign Relations Press, 1993), p. 100.

[6] Andrew J. Goodpaster, "Further Reins on Nuclear Arms: Next Steps by Nuclear Powers," Atlantic Council, Washington, D.C., August 1993.

[7] See Solly Zuckerman, *Nuclear Illusions and Reality* (New York: Viking, 1982), p. 70; and *Sunday Times* (London), February 21, 1982.

[8] Quoted in *Congressional Record*, July 1, 1981.

[9] See the *Washington Post*, April 12, 1982.

[10] *Boston Globe*, July 16, 1994.

[11] Robert S. McNamara, "The Military Role of Nuclear Weapons," *Foreign Affairs*, Fall 1983, p. 79.

[12] See William Perry's statement to the Stimson Center, September 20, 1994; and Department of Defense press briefing, September 22, 1994.

[13] The U.S. Congress is currently considering legislation that would direct the Administration to develop and deploy anti-ballistic missile defenses. If such legislation were to be passed, it would very likely result in an indefinite postponement of ratification of the Bush-Yeltsin agreement by both the Russian Duma and the U.S. Senate.

[14] "Insofar as practicable" refers to the necessity of maintaining protection against "breakout," or acquisition of weapons by terrorists. The elimination of nuclear weapons could be accomplished in a series of steps, as both General Goodpaster and I have suggested.

[15] Option 3 would permit the nuclear powers to fulfill their obligations under Article VI of the recently approved Nuclear Non-Proliferation Treaty. Article VI states that "Each of the Parties to the Treaty undertakes to pursue negotiations in good faith on effective measures relating to the cessation of the nuclear arms race at an early date *and to nuclear disarmament . . .* " [emphasis added].

NEXT STEPS IN ARMS CONTROL:
HOW FAR, HOW FAST?

RYUKICHI IMAI

The context of nuclear power has changed many times during and after the Cold War. Now that fifty years have passed since the debut of nuclear power, it is useful to re-evaluate its possible role in the next century.

Back when splitting the atom was seen as an inexpensive means of protecting Western Europe, nuclear weapons were treated as powerful but ordinary bombs. Only after the Soviet Union developed its own nuclear arsenal did serious work begin on defining nuclear strategic doctrines.

In the context of the superpower global confrontation, any third party with independent nuclear weapons would be a serious nuisance. (Nuclear weapons in the 1960s were primitive devices that could be built by any competent country with an automobile industry and a national R&D expenditure of 0.5 percent of the gross national product.)

The first step against nuclear proliferation was the ban on weapons testing. Immediately after the Cuban missile crisis, the 1963 Partial Test Ban Treaty (PTBT) was concluded. After the PTBT, serious negotiations began on nuclear non-proliferation. The Eighteen Nations Disarmament Commission (later the Conference on Disarmament) was created in Geneva. In 1968 it produced a draft of the NPT.

NPT EXTENSION CONFERENCE IN 1995

The rapid development of the two superpowers' nuclear arsenals, delivery vehicles, launching platforms, and command/control systems surprised the world. In the 1970s, the United States and the Soviet Union were technically so superior that no third party could meaningfully interfere in the negotiations on anti-ballistic missiles, the multiple independently targetable re-entry vehicles (MIRVs), or the respective windows of vulnerability.

The 1995 NPT extension conference avoided creating a vacuum in which countries like Iran, Libya, or North Korea could legitimately possess nuclear weapons. But it did create a climate in which second-rate nuclear weapons states would continue to upgrade their (sea-based) nuclear capabilities. Consequently, the future of a comprehensive test ban looks uncertain, and opportunity was lost to convince the world

NUCLEAR WEAPONS OF THE WORLD

	1990	1994	2003
United States	**12,718**	**8,258**	**3,450/3,500**
ICBM	2,450	2,090	450/500
SLBM	5,760	2,688	1,680
Bomber mounted	4,508	3,480	1,320
U.S.S.R./Russia	**10,799**	**8,943**	**3,499**
ICBM	6,612	4,963	1,005
SLBM	2,804	2,544	1,696
Bomber mounted	1,363	1,436	798
United Kingdom		**200**	
SLBM		100	
Bomber mounted		100	
France		**554**	
Surface/surface		90	
SLBM		384	
Bomber mounted		80	
China		**448**	
Surface/surface		100	
SLBM		48	
Bomber mounted		150	
Others		150	

Note: ICBM=intercontinental ballistic missiles.
SLBM=submarine-launched ballistic missiles.

Sources: *Nuclear Weapons Data Book*, *Arms Control Today*, and *SIPRI Yearbook* (Stockholm International Peace Research Institute).

that the Cold War notion of nuclear-war fighting as a serious option has been terminated. Given the uncertainty surrounding START II ratification, the potential for nuclear disarmament as a whole appears unclear. Other items, such as negative security assurances and cutoff of fissile material production, are mere repetition of the agenda items in Geneva.

The table above shows large gaps in the quantity and quality of nuclear arsenals among the United States, Russia, and the three other nuclear-weapon states. (If Israel has 100 weapons, as reported, its only distinction from other declared nuclear-weapon states is official NWS status under the NPT and modern underwater-launch capabilities.) Even if ways are found to solve the vast political and legal problems, implementation of START II is a difficult technical process involving storage, transportation, and dismantling of nuclear warheads. Because maximum dismantling capacity of both the United States and Russia is about 2,000 per year, at least ten years are required to reach targets. The U.S. posture of regarding plutonium only as radioactive waste, and not an energy-valuable reactor fuel, discourages Russia from dismantling activities.

ROGUE STATES AND TERRORISTS

Fifty years after Hiroshima, we have come to realize that nuclear warheads are too destructive and belong to an era of unconditional surrender and indiscriminate destruction. Still it is awkward for superpowers to have to worry about rogue states or terrorists who might steal a bomb or create one (real, fake, or fizzle) from reactor-grade plutonium.

This is even more true after Saddam Hussein's attempts to create weapons of mass destruction by purchasing pieces of the technology. Concern is no longer about major states (as the NPT intended), or the emerging Third World countries (concerns of the late 1970s). The world today is worried about the physical security of Pu-239 rich plutonium from American and Russian dismantled weapons and other remnants of the Cold War. A greatly increased load on safeguards and other verification procedures requires new and careful review both of processes and institutions.

The IAEA safeguards were designed as a deterrence against military diversion of nuclear material from peaceful uses. With the increasing worldwide volume of nuclear fuel and plutonium, the IAEA should switch its emphasis from material accountancy to containment and surveillance. Like-minded countries with technical and financial capabilities to utilize modern remote-sensing technologies could initiate a new system; for example, an expansion of "national technical means" verification into a worldwide system that serves in implementation of disarmament and non-proliferation, and possibly monitors environmental contamination for everyone, including the NPT nuclear-weapon states. However, such a body could not begin to function under the United Nations—with 187 member countries, each with a vote.

During the transition from Cold War confrontation to a new framework for peaceful uses of nuclear energy, more transparency is required. Difficulties lie in the sensitivity of weapons-related information, materials, and equipment, but excessive secrecy will discourage the necessary cooperation. Arguably, the United States and Russia would need to sustain respectable weapons-industry levels—if only to ensure the safe maintenance of START II warheads. Meanwhile, the targeting doctrine for 3,000-3,500 warheads has to be clarified as deterrence or otherwise, if only to justify budgets. France, China, India, and Israel also have to be more accountable for their actions and inactions, while South Africa's confession of six bombs should be carefully examined, with the findings published.

Only after these points have been addressed will the world be ready to entertain a meaningful START III or take steps toward a nuclear-free world. To "put the genie back into the bottle," something other than deterrence theory, theater missile defense arrangements, or IAEA material accountancy needs to emerge as a basis of confidence-building measures.

NUCLEAR ENERGY IN THE 21ST CENTURY

Eisenhower's 1953 "Atoms for Peace" proposal was welcomed by a world in desperate need of energy for reconstruction and development. But cheap and abundant energy was provided in the 1960s by oil from the Middle East. Only with the 1973 oil crisis did everyone turn to nuclear energy, so that at one point combined world programs for nuclear power generation by the year 2000 were projected to reach some 3.5 billion kw (actual capacity in 1995 was 356 million kw in operation and 56 million kw under construction).

Nuclear power generation of 3.5 billion kw requires a bulk of plutonium fuel, but in 1977 the United States began campaigning for denial of plutonium for civilian purposes. In 1983, when the United States and the Soviet Union were in heated negotiations over medium-range ballistic missiles in Europe, anti-nuclear movements in Western Europe combined forces with the radical political left and increased their clout. In 1986, crude-oil prices plunged. These and other factors made further large-scale nuclear power programs in Western Europe unlikely in the late 1980s and preclude them for the time being.

Throughout the Cold War, East Asia did not have its own counterparts of the Conference on Security and Cooperation in Europe (CSCE), the Western European Union (WEU), the North Atlantic Treaty Organization (NATO), or the North American Free Trade Agreement (NAFTA). Attempts were made to create similar regimes, including the Asia-Pacific Economic Cooperation (APEC) forum, the East Asian Economic Cooperation (EAEC) forum, and the U.S.–Japan Mutual Security Agreement. But it is difficult to predict Asia's economic and security structure in the next century, given its mix of a strong economy like Japan; emerging tigers such as Singapore, Hong Kong, Taiwan, and South Korea; and the potential giant economic power that is China.

The United States became a Pacific power after its expansionism ended with the acquisition of the Philippines. The United States was always attentive to China and to its Open Door policy as a matter of trade and humanitarian concerns. Today, looking at U.S.–China relations, it is not clear what grand design lies behind various U.S. moves, nor is it clear whether China has any coherent strategy of its own.

The 20th century saw rapid progress in science and technology. Along with atomic energy, this brought high-speed communication systems, cheap mass transportation, and a better quality of life—and thus a larger world population and concomitant environmental contamination. By the year 2040, the earth will need to support ten billion people, of whom over 25 percent will live in East Asia. There is no question that the region will require a very large supply of energy.

China's extensive burning of coal aggravates the already high level of acid rain in Japan. Increased use of hydrocarbon fuels also aggravates problems associated with the greenhouse effect. According to the 1994 Framework Convention on Climatic Changes, the world has to limit CO_2 emissions to the 1990 level. This does not appeal to the developing countries. The developed world may have to find new, sophisticated, and probably more expensive energy resources, and release liquid and gaseous hydrocarbons for use by the developing world.

One solution to the world's energy needs is to "go nuclear," as China has started to do. It is operating Chinsan-1 station (350 MWe), based on its own nuclear submarine technology, and it has started operation of two large Guandong Daya Bay plants with French technology. China is reportedly planning 20 million kw of nuclear power by the year 2010, and 40-60 million kw by 2020. This is frightening, as Chinese standards for nuclear safety are unclear. Should there be a Chinese "Chernobyl," westerly winds would carry a large amount of radioactive material to Japan.

China, as one of the NPT nuclear-weapon states, has rights to use plutonium as fuel, which it plans to do. A crucial issue to be decided in the near future is where to locate fuel-cycle centers in East Asia. By extending the NPT indefinitely without conditions on the nuclear-weapon states, the world has no effective means left to deal with the China that may emerge as a nuclear giant in the post-Deng era. A similar concern exists about the Russian far east.

Considering the problem of converting military industry into civilian industry, and the global trend of seeking out new markets for conventional weapons, there are good reasons to look for improved policy coordination among countries in disarmament and non-proliferation matters, with respect to both conventional weapons and weapons of mass destruction. It is disturbing that the replacement of the Coordinating Committee on Multilateral Export Controls (COCOM) technology-transfer system cannot be agreed upon despite prolonged discussions and negotiations.

U.S. NUCLEAR STRATEGY: ADAPTING TO THE NEW WORLD DISORDER

STEVEN E. MILLER

During the Cold War, U.S. nuclear policy was overwhelmingly oriented toward deterring Soviet nuclear and conventional attacks on the United States and its allies. In support of this objective, the United States maintained an enormous, diverse, rapidly modernizing, highly alerted nuclear force; and it adopted an ambitious nuclear doctrine that generated requirements for nuclear first-use and retaliatory counterforce options. With the collapse of the Soviet Union and—equally important—the rapid transformation of Washington's relations with Russia, the rationale for this vast physical and conceptual nuclear infrastructure disappeared.

Consequently, what has unfolded over the past several years has been a process of reconsideration and adjustment of U.S. nuclear policy. This process has not produced enough change fast enough to please every critic.[1]

THE DECLINING SALIENCE OF NUCLEAR WEAPONS

During the Cold War, debates and concerns about U.S. nuclear forces, doctrine, and arms control policy occupied center stage in public discourse on and political battling over U.S. security policy. This is much less true today. While nuclear issues remain important, they are far less central and salient than they used to be. As the Department of Defense's annual report for 1995 puts it, "Nuclear weapons are playing a smaller role in U.S. security than at any other time in the nuclear age."[2]

THE PERSISTENCE OF A NUCLEAR THREAT

The reduced role of nuclear weapons in U.S. security policy does not imply that nuclear threats have ceased to be a factor in U.S. security calculations. On the contrary, with the waning of the Soviet challenge, the threat posed by nuclear weapons (and other weapons of mass destruction) is at the top of the list of U.S. security concerns. The Department of Defense has stated clearly that, of the dangers facing the United States in the post–Cold War era, "the one that most urgently and directly threatens American interests is the proliferation of weapons of mass destruction."[3]

The new nuclear threat has several dimensions, in contrast to the Cold War preoccupation with the threat of Soviet nuclear attack.

- **The re-emergence of a nuclear threat from Moscow.** Russia still possesses the largest nuclear arsenal that could threaten the United States. That arsenal is not a great source of concern as long as Russia remains benign and its relations with the United States are friendly. But should developments in Russia turn sour and a hostile leadership take power in Moscow, nuclear capabilities would pose a massive nuclear threat to the United States. This "residual" nuclear threat from Russia looms large in current U.S. thinking about its own nuclear deterrent requirements. Over time, evidence that a benign Russia is certain to emerge from the present political transformation would cause this fear to lose its force.

- **The possible emergence of a Chinese nuclear threat to the United States.** To date, China has had little capability to threaten nuclear attack against the territory of the United States (although it has long had the ability to strike Japan with nuclear weapons). This could change in the coming decade. China's rapid economic growth and vigorous military modernization could give it a growing intercontinental nuclear capability. As Secretary of Defense William Perry has commented, China "has the potential to increase the size and capability of its strategic nuclear arsenal significantly over the next decade."[4] The Clinton Administration feels the need to take this possibility into account in its nuclear policy. Over time, evidence of significant growth and modernization of Chinese nuclear forces would cause this concern to increase in importance as a factor in determining U.S. policy.

- **The threat of nuclear proliferation.** The United States is urgently concerned about the further spread of nuclear weapons to other hostile powers. President Clinton said at the United Nations in September 1993 that, "If we do not stem the proliferation of the world's deadliest weapons, no democracy can feel secure." Secretary of Defense Perry has identified proliferation as the most important problem faced by the Department of Defense.[5] Proliferation can threaten U.S. allies, complicate U.S. intervention with conventional forces, and raise the risk of nuclear attacks against the territory of the United States by states other than Russia and China.

- *The risk of nuclear leakage from the former Soviet Union.* An unprecedented threat arises from the possibility that nuclear weapons or fissile material may leak out of the former Soviet Union. This would greatly undermine the international non-proliferation regime and could contribute disastrously to the spread of nuclear weapons. A rupture of the Russian nuclear custodial system would make nuclear weapons, or the materials to make them, available to anyone who had the capacity to pay. By divorcing nuclear acquisition from the technical and industrial capacity of states, large-scale nuclear leakage would greatly increase the risk of nuclear terrorism; terrorist groups could buy on the nuclear black market as easily as states. Hence, the United States (as well as Japan and all other states with an interest in preventing nuclear proliferation) has an enormous stake in the integrity and effectiveness of a Russian nuclear custodial system functioning in extremely turbulent conditions.[6] Indeed, FBI Director Louis Freeh has identified the problem of nuclear leakage as "the greatest long-term threat to the security of the United States."[7]

Thus, though the pervasive Soviet nuclear threat no longer exists, nuclear threats continue to figure prominently in U.S. security policy.

ABANDONMENT OF THE COLD WAR NUCLEAR POSTURE

The impact of these new nuclear threats on U.S. policy has been considerable, but they do not warrant or justify anything resembling the Cold War nuclear posture formerly maintained by the United States. Accordingly, many of the patterns and attributes previously associated with U.S. nuclear forces have been, or are being, reversed or abandoned.[8] U.S. nuclear forces have already shrunk substantially, with further cuts slated for the years ahead. Whereas widespread force modernization was once the norm, modernization has now slowed to a standstill. Whereas previously the force was kept on hairtrigger alert, today it has been substantially de-alerted. Whereas not so long ago the U.S. nuclear arsenal contained a bewildering diversity of forces, today it is considerably less diverse. Though some remain disappointed that more has not been done, the changes that have already occurred are striking.

RETAINING A SUBSTANTIAL NUCLEAR ARSENAL

The post–Cold War U.S. nuclear force may be smaller, sleeker, and safer. But it is nevertheless still the case that present plans call for the United States to possess a substantial nuclear force for the foreseeable future. This reflects a judgment that the United States requires an ample deterrent force, both to "hedge" against potential threats and to fulfill its extended deterrence obligations to allies (obligations that have been explicitly reaffirmed in the Clinton Administration's Nuclear Posture Review). The planned force is essentially a START II force— that is, it is a force that will go down to the limits required by START II, but no lower. The question of how much lower the United States can and should go is certain to be debated in the years ahead.

"DEFENSE BY OTHER MEANS"

During the Cold War, the United States sought to neutralize the Soviet nuclear threat primarily by building its own nuclear deterrent force; arms control played a role in containing the nuclear arms race in some respects, but it was not a primary mechanism for dealing with the nuclear threat. Some of the new nuclear threats have the distinctive property that they cannot be fully or adequately addressed simply by the maintenance of nuclear deterrent forces. This is true of the proliferation and leakage threats.

Hence, a substantial new emphasis in U.S. policy is on programs that seek to deal with these threats via different avenues than nuclear deterrence—an approach described by the Department of Defense as "defense by other means." There are two prominent examples of this: the Counterproliferation Initiative and the Cooperative Threat Reduction Program.

Notes

[1] See, for example, the criticism in William Arkin, "A Tale of Two Franks," *Bulletin of Atomic Scientists,* March-April 1995, p. 80. Arkin complains of the Clinton Administration's nuclear posture review that "mid-level bureaucrats and one-star generals were allowed to push through the predictable result. Stagnation was assured."

[2] Secretary of Defense William Perry, *Annual Report to the President and the Congress,* Washington D.C.: USGPO, February 1995, p. 83.

[3] Office of the Deputy Secretary of Defense, *Report on Nonproliferation and Counterproliferation Activities and Programs,* May 1994, p. 2.

[4] *DoD Annual Report,* 1995, p. 163. Perry's new emphasis on the potential Chinese nuclear threat is highlighted in Dunbar Lockwood, "DOD Report Sheds Light on Nuclear Policy, Forces," *Arms Control Today,* April 1995, p. 21.

[5] Both quoted in *Report on Nonproliferation and Counterproliferation Activities and Programs,* p. 2.

[6] See, for example, *DoD Annual Report, 1995*, p. 64. A detailed analysis of this problem is Graham Allison, Owen Cote, Richard Falkenrath, and Steven Miller, "Containing Loose Nukes: A Strategy for Defending the United States from Nuclear Weapons," CSIA Discussion Paper, May 1995.

[7] Quoted in Charles Hanley, "Weapons Smuggling: Nuclear Black Market Greatest Threat to the Security of the United States," *Cincinnati Enquirer*, March 26, 1995.

[8] For more detail, see Steven E. Miller, "Dismantling the Edifice: Strategic Nuclear Forces in the Post-Soviet Era," in Charles F. Hermann, ed., *American Defense Annual*, 1994 (New York: Lexington Books, 1994), pp. 650-84.

U.S. NUCLEAR STRATEGY: ADAPTING TO THE NEW WORLD DISORDER

SATOSHI MORIMOTO

CHARACTERISTICS OF U.S. NUCLEAR STRATEGY

The United States has maintained the doctrine of deterrence as its fundamental nuclear strategy since the beginning of the Cold War. Under this strategy, the United States deters nuclear war by displaying the will and capability to retaliate against any country attempting to launch a first-strike nuclear attack against it. Though the names used to describe U.S. nuclear strategy may change, the basic concept of deterrence remains the same.

To implement an effective deterrent strategy, the United States must: (1) maintain a highly resilient capability to inflict unacceptable damage on any country launching a first strike; (2) have the firm resolve to retaliate in the event deterrence fails while making clear the actions it aims to deter; and (3) ensure that potential adversaries are aware of the U.S. resolve and the reasonableness of its stance.

U.S. nuclear war capability is inevitably related to its nuclear strategy. Although logic dictates that a nuclear strategy must first be established and nuclear war capability subsequently developed to implement the strategy, improvement and modernization of U.S. nuclear war capability are not necessarily based on U.S. nuclear strategy. Nevertheless, nuclear strategy and war capability are closely related. In the background of this relationship was an important priority of balancing U.S. nuclear capability with that of the Soviet Union, while striving to tip the balance in favor of the United States.

The balance of nuclear war capability between the United States and the Soviet Union shifted from overwhelming U.S. dominance in the 1950s to rough parity from the end of the 1960s to the mid-1970s, as the quality and size of the Soviet nuclear arsenal improved. The United States further lost its dominance in various fields between the 1970s and early 1980s as the Soviet Union modernized its weapons.

The Soviet Union appeared to pose its greatest threat to the United States at the beginning of the 1980s. Taking office at this juncture, the Reagan Administration promoted a plan for modernizing the U.S. strategic nuclear arsenal. The U.S. Strategic Defense Initiative, in particular, imposed enormous economic burdens on the Soviet Union in carrying out is strategic nuclear plans. The efforts made in the first term of the Reagan Administration gradually yielded fruit during its second term and led to a recovery of self-confidence in the U.S. government. This self-confidence motivated the U.S. to conduct bilateral arms control talks with the Soviet Union, such as those on the Intermediate Nuclear Forces (INF) Treaty and the Strategic Arms Reduction Treaty (START) in the middle of the 1980s. The balance of nuclear war capability steadily inclined toward the United States in the late 1980s as the development of strategic nuclear weapon systems progressed at an unprecedented speed.

The United States has improved its nuclear war and nuclear deterrent capabilities since the days of the Cold War, while continuing to participate in arms control talks to maintain strategic stability for itself and its allies. Noteworthy U.S. accomplishments include the conclusion of nuclear arms control agreements on the INF and those on START I and START II.

Strategic stability refers to a situation in which the capabilities of strategic nuclear attack and strategic defense are balanced between two parties to deter nuclear war, and this deterrence functions to eliminate any move on either side to launch a preemptive attack.

If the conventional warfare capabilities of the United States and the Soviet Union were to be in balance as a whole, and nuclear war capabilities were also to be balanced at a low level, each country would have less incentive to start a war and thus strategic stability would be enhanced. Achieving strategic stability requires: (1) controlling strategic nuclear warfare capabilities while improving their resilience; (2) building firm and reliable strategic defense capability; and (3) maintaining balanced strategic nuclear war and strategic defense capabilities. The purpose of the strategic arms reduction talks was to achieve these targets through an arms control agreement. In this way, U.S. nuclear strategy has always been governed by the relations among balanced nuclear strategies, improvement of nuclear warfare capabilities, and arms control policies. However, the ultimate purpose of U.S. nuclear strategy was to maintain global strategic stability by maintaining a nuclear war capability superior to that of the Soviet Union.

CHANGES IN THE STRATEGIC ENVIRONMENT
AFTER THE COLD WAR

The end of the Cold War prompted the United States to reexamine its nuclear strategy. The following is a review of changes in the strategic environment brought about by the end of the Cold War and their impact on U.S. nuclear strategy.

128

Collapse of the Soviet Union

The most conspicuous change in the strategic environment was the collapse of the Soviet Union and the subsequent democratization and reforms toward a market economy in the states of the former Soviet Union.

With the collapse of the Soviet Union, the United States lost its opponent, and its nuclear strategy was influenced by the disappearance of ideological conflict and military opposition between the Eastern and Western blocs.

Having inherited most of the assets of the former Soviet Union, Russia nevertheless maintains strategic nuclear war capabilities sufficient to rival those of the United States. Russian military doctrine since the end of the Cold War indicates that Russia's nuclear strategy is basically not different from that of the former Soviet Union. Albeit slowly, Russia is continuing to modernize its intercontinental ballistic missiles (ICBMs) and to increase the production of its submarine-launched ballistic missiles (SLBMs).

The opaque nature of Russian politics and the rise of totalitarian conservative forces in Russia create doubts about whether democratization and reform will succeed.

Arms Control Agreements and Nuclear Arms Reduction

Another change that has influenced nuclear strategy is the adjustment and curtailment of U.S. and Russian nuclear war capability in the post–Cold War period. By the end of 1992, the United States and Russia had withdrawn all tactical nuclear weapons carried at sea and on dual-capable airplanes, as well as almost all other categories of tactical nuclear weapons. Having negotiated to eliminate intermediate-range nuclear weapons, based on the INF Treaty concluded in December 1987, both countries eliminated all such weapons by the end of 1991.

With respect to strategic nuclear weapons, the United States and the Soviet Union had intended to implement a process of reducing the number of vehicles for strategic nuclear weapons to 1,600, and the number of warheads to 6,000. With the collapse of the Soviet Union at the end of 1991 and the advent of the Commonwealth of Independent States (CIS), the Soviet arsenal of strategic nuclear weapons was dispersed among Russia, Belarus, Kazakhstan, and Ukraine.

In December 1994, Ukraine ratified the NPT. Thus the START I agreement entered into force. The United States and Russia had promoted the disarmament process even before the agreement was ratified. It is expected that START I will further expedite nuclear arms reduction. On the other hand, the future of START II remains open until Russia ratifies it.

Nuclear Weapons Counter-Proliferation After the Cold War

The issue that has had the greatest influence on nuclear strategy after the Cold War is the proliferation of weapons of mass destruction. Several events since 1990, involving proliferation of weapons of mass destruction, and nuclear weapons in particular, have affected post–Cold War U.S. nuclear strategy.

The first such event was the finding by the IAEA team, which inspected Iraqi nuclear facilities after the 1990 Gulf crisis, that the weapons development program had survived. This raised serious questions about the IAEA inspection system and the NPT system it is based upon, since it was found that a Third World country could secretly develop nuclear weapons while participating in the NPT regime. In this sense, the case of Iraq cast doubt on the viability of post–Cold War counter-proliferation systems.

Second is a series of events related to the collapse of the Soviet Union. Problems arose with the transport, storage, and dismantling of nuclear weapons in the CIS countries. Since Russia had the capability to dismantle only 2,000 warheads a year, it became necessary to provide Russia with funds, materials, and engineers to dismantle all the weapons transfered from the other CIS countries. Russia also lacked the capability to transport and store these weapons safely.

The dismantling of nuclear weapons was never considered when they were developed and manufactured. The disarming and dismantling of nuclear weapons raises fears that the related technologies and engineers could be transfered to other countries, and the handling and storage of the enriched uranium and plutonium from dismantled weapons poses a serious problem.

Third, evidence of Third World states in possession of weapons of mass destruction, formerly confined to Iraq, North Korea, and some other countries, has grown. This problem existed even during the Cold War, when both the Eastern and Western blocs were preoccupied with threats from each other and were not sufficiently aware of the threat from regional powers. Now some countries outside the NPT community have apparently developed and are in possession of weapons of mass destruction, including nuclear weapons. Through technological developments and commercial transfers of arms-related technologies and materials, it is no longer difficult to develop and manufacture weapons of mass destruction or to acquire the materials and facilities required for developing them.

Suspicions are spreading about North Korea. South Africa, which had a nuclear development program and possessed nuclear weapons, joined the NPT community in 1991 and declared that it had dismantled these weapons. Israel, which is outside the NPT community, has apparently succeeded in developing nuclear weapons without conducting nuclear-test explosions and is reportedly in possession of a number of such weapons. India and Pakistan, which are also outside the NPT community, allegedly have the capability to develop nuclear weapons. It appears that other Third World countries, such as Iran and Brazil, are also beginning to develop nuclear weapons.

U.S. NUCLEAR WAR CAPABILITY AFTER THE COLD WAR

Review of U.S. Nuclear Strategy

Background. The U.S. review of its nuclear strategy after the Cold War was completely different from past reviews when the United States was concerned only with nuclear deterrence against the Soviet Union.

The purpose of the first review after the Cold War was to seek an answer to an important basic question: What is the purpose and role of the U.S. nuclear deterrent? Although Russia remained a nuclear superpower, it no longer would pose a nuclear threat if progress in its democratization continued. However, after the election of the Russian Parliament in December 1993, the possibility arose that totalitarian conservatism could take root in Russia and crush or retard democratization. The United States was obliged to take account of this possibility.

The United States also had to take into account the problem of nuclear weapons proliferation. It had to consider whether it could deter further proliferation by possessing its own nuclear arsenal. In other words, should the United States use its nuclear weapons and their deterrent capability to protect its own interests and those of its allies if Iran, Iraq, North Korea, Libya, India, Pakistan, and other Third World countries came into possession of nuclear weapons? Another question was whether nuclear weapons could deter threats arising from biological and chemical weapons.

In addition to changes in the international environment, domestic changes had to be considered. Congressional desire to cut the defense budget increased under financial pressure generated by the rapidly rising national debt. With the end of the Cold War, the U.S. public began to think it was possible to reduce the strategic nuclear war capability, and sentiment grew in favor of greater efforts to reduce armaments. The public became less aware of the significant role of nuclear deterrence than it had been in the past. Although public opinion alone did not change U.S. security policy, the change in public opinion began to affect government policies.

"Leading and Hedging." The first post–Cold War review of U.S. nuclear strategy was described as the Nuclear Posture Review (NPR). However, its findings were not presented in a formal report, but in press

onference statements in September 1994—by Defense Secretary William Perry and Deputy Secretary John Deutch—discussing the evolution of new concepts concerning the U.S. nuclear posture. These do not amount to a new nuclear strategy. The concepts of U.S. nuclear strategy may have been discussed, but without reaching well-defined conclusions.

The NPR contains several underlying concepts of U.S. nuclear strategy. The **first** is the role of nuclear weapons in the post–Cold War era, which is to: (1) maintain deterrence against various categories and forms of threat; (2) prevent Russian nuclear dominance in view of the fact that Russia still has nuclear weapons; and (3) prevent proliferation of weapons of mass destruction. The goal of preventing Russian nuclear dominance is easily understood because it is consistent with traditional nuclear deterrence thinking. But whether nuclear arms can deter other threats and prevent proliferation is doubtful.

What is meant by various categories and forms of threat? Does this imply that nuclear weapons will be launched if threats arise from conventional weapons, ballistic missiles, or biological and chemical weapons? How can nuclear weapons be deployed to deter such threats? These questions pose serious issues about the role of nuclear weapons as a deterrent to "various threats."

The concept of the U.S. nuclear arsenal playing a counter-proliferation role is even more problematical. What does using U.S. nuclear weapons to prevent the proliferation of weapons of mass destruction mean? How can the U.S. nuclear arsenal be used to prevent another country from attempting to acquire nuclear weapons?

The **second** concept of nuclear strategy underlying the Nuclear Posture Review is the notion that deterrence can be assured by steadfastly maintaining a highly resilient and dependable capability to hold at risk the urgent national interests and potential values of a country that poses a threat.

The United States regards Russia, with its at the very least 12,000 strategic and tactical warheads, as the primary target of its deterrent strategy. The course of social, political, and economic reforms in Russia remains uncertain. The United States should be able to exercise nuclear deterrence in the event that democratization fails in Russia and an antagonistic government emerges to compromise the process of bilateral arms control. This is essentially a "hedging" strategy.

Another view is that nuclear deterrence is the fundamental basis of U.S. national security and, therefore, its nuclear capability should be superior to that of any other country. By maintaining its nuclear dominance, it is argued, the United States can reduce nuclear arms on a global scale, including Russia's. This view implies that the United States should maintain its dominance as a nuclear superpower. U.S. nuclear strategy after the Cold War has combined these strategies for "leading and hedging."

But this approach poses several problems. First, global disarmament will not progress as long as the United States maintains a strategy of leading. China and France will try to catch up with the United States and Russia. Thus the arms race will continue. If a Comprehensive Test Ban Treaty (CTBT) prohibits all nuclear explosions, the pace of nuclear weapons modernization will slow substantially after the treaty is concluded and implemented. In the meantime, however, nuclear powers will continue to modernize their nuclear weapon systems and this will make it more difficult to hold comprehensive disarmament talks.

Second, it is not clear at what point the United States should stop hedging on the outcome in Russia. Russia will be suspicious of the United States as long as the United States maintains a hedging strategy. Even if START II is ratified by Russia, the U.S. hedging strategy will be an obstacle to its implementation and to the beginning of negotiations on START III.

Third, the relationship with Russia is accorded the highest priority in U.S. nuclear strategy, whether through leading or hedging. Therefore, some fear that U.S. nuclear warfare capability is not effective for dealing with issues of proliferation or threats arising elsewhere. In particular, the issue of non-proliferation, which is one of the most serious and important issues today, will not be resolved with U.S. efforts toward arms control. In the end, it seems that the nuclear warfare capabilities of the United States cannot prevent the proliferation of nuclear arms.

Nuclear Arsenal: Review and Change

First, the United States has modified the composition of its nuclear arsenal since the end of the Cold War. By October 1994, the United States, which had been reducing its nuclear arsenal since before START I was implemented, had destroyed 47 percent of the approximately 90,000 warheads it possessed in 1988. The Nuclear Posture Review outlines the new composition of the nuclear arsenal under the START II framework.

As for the non-strategic nuclear arsenal, intermediate-range nuclear weapons were eliminated under the INF Treaty, and some tactical nuclear weapons were also eliminated under the Bush Initiative. The number of warheads in the U.S. nuclear arsenal was reduced by 90 percent from the 1988 level.

Second, changes have been made in the nuclear-alert posture and safety-control procedures. The United States has changed its command-post structure and reduced the operational tempo of its strategic nuclear warfare and global airborne command systems. It has also changed the peacetime alert posture of strategic bombers and reduced the number of submarines in operation. However, the ICBM alert posture continues.

Army and Marine Corps personnel have been reassigned from duties related to nuclear weapons. Nuclear weapons are not deployed to the surface Navy on a permanent basis. The number of personnel with access to nuclear weapons or their control has been reduced by 70 percent and the number of nuclear storage locations by more than 75 percent. The United States and Russia agreed at the October 1994 summit talks to eliminate nuclear warheads after ratification of START II in order to relax the alert posture of all nuclear-weapon delivery systems.

The United States improved safety control over nuclear weapons, expedited introduction of coded locking devices for submarine missiles, and upgraded locking devices on bombers and silo-based missiles. While making great changes in the nuclear command and control systems, as well as the information systems, the United States has maintained its C_3I (Command, Control, Communication, Intelligence) organization for the purpose of retaining a credible deterrence.

The third change is in counter-proliferation activity. Although counter-proliferation may not seem immediately relevant to the U.S. nuclear posture, the extent to which the United States can promote non-proliferation will have great influence, since counter-proliferation action will reduce potential nuclear threats the United States may confront.

U.S. counter-proliferation activities focus in particular on Russia and the other CIS countries. This focus is represented in the "Nunn-Lugar" Cooperative Threat Reduction programs, under which $1.2 billion will be spent to provide these countries with personnel, facilities, equipment, materials, and parts to deactivate, dismantle, transport, and store nuclear weapons. Agreements on a number of projects have been signed to this end since 1993. This counter-proliferation program has contributed to improving the U.S. nuclear posture.

Arms Control Policies

Proliferation has been the most important arms control issue for the United States after the Cold War. The United States advocated an unconditional and indefinite extension of the NPT, and it achieved success in May 1995. Now it is preparing for early conclusion of the CTBT and for a cut-off convention on fissile material for weapons use. It is also making efforts to increase the number of participating countries and to strengthen information-gathering functions to implement the Missile Technology Control Regime.

The non-proliferation issue, which has the highest priority for the United States, is being pursued to prevent proliferation in the countries that formerly made up the Soviet Union.

134

Agreement on the CTBT is the second highest U.S. priority (after the indefinite extension of the NPT). After serious governmental discussions on nuclear experiments, the United States decided in August 1995 that it will not conduct any experiment that involves a nuclear explosion, and it is encouraging early conclusion of the CTBT.

Nuclear disarmament is another important arms control issue for the United States. The target for the time being is to implement START I and obtain Russian ratification of START II. As for implementation of START I, the United States is concerned not only about the process of de-activating and dismantling Russian strategic nuclear weapons, but also about the transfer to Russia and dismantling of the strategic nuclear weapon systems now in Belarus, Kazakhstan, and Ukraine.

Once ratification of START II is within reach, the United States and Russia will be able to enter the next stage of arms control negotiations. The purpose, participants, objectives, and target of the next round of talks are not yet known.

In order to maintain its commitments to its allies—while reducing its strategic nuclear weapons arsenal to the minimum level required to protect national interests and enhance strategic stability, the United States must attain the levels agreed to in START I and II as soon as possible. It should set targets in subsequent arms control negotiations while considering conditions in Russia and the implementation status of the START agreements.

DENUCLEARIZATION INITIATIVES:
WILL THE 'BIG BOYS' PLAY?

JOHN E. ENDICOTT

W hen considering the question of whether or not the major powers in Northeast Asia will participate in various proposals for restricting the use or the existence of nuclear weapons in the region, the first inclination is to turn to the issue of Chinese, Russian, Japanese, and U.S. policy toward non-proliferation. These are the 'big boys.' That, of course, leaves us terribly exposed as to the question of the policies of North and South Korea and Taiwan. The question of Mongolia's position became clear in October 1993 with its public declaration of a statewide nuclear-free zone.

The specific concept that is considered here is a proposal for a limited nuclear-free zone (LNFZ) in Northeast Asia that would involve all the weapon-possessing states of the region (Russia, China, and the United States) as well as their neighbors. First proposed as a zone centered on the Demilitarized Zone (DMZ) of the Korean Peninsula that would exclude all nuclear weapons, it has evolved through informal and formal discussions with the security communities concerned to a zone more elliptical in nature that would also include part of Alaska and would initially focus on tactical nuclear weapons only. An agency for oversight and agreement verification, located possibly in Hiroshima or Nagasaki, is at the heart of the concept and would become the first functioning multilateral security organization in Northeast Asia.

CHINA: PLAYER OR NOT?

A t first, it might be easy to jump to a conclusion on the question of China's participation. China is very sensitive about its sovereignty, and any actions that might appear to compromise the notion of an independent China that has emerged from one hundred years of colonial spoilage and almost fifty years of competition with the West would be subject to immediate rejection by the Beijing government. China has, however, taken some very interesting steps with regard to non-proliferation.

China has articulated a policy of "no first use" since it obtained its nuclear weapons capability. "China will never be the first to use nuclear weapons," has become an often repeated statement that is generally taken to mean that China forswears the first use of nuclear weapons in any future confrontation. China is a signatory to the Nuclear Non-Proliferation Treaty (NPT) and participated in the NPT Review Conference in 1995. It has practiced, to a surprising extent, unilateral restraint in the number of nuclear weapons it has produced and deployed, and it has indicated a willingness to join the Comprehensive Nuclear Test Ban Treaty (CTBT) in 1996, once the currently scheduled nuclear tests are concluded.

When the concept of a limited nuclear-free zone was addressed in Beijing in March 1992, it was held to be the height of folly by some Chinese critics as it was seen to be a demonstration of attempts by the United States to extend and consolidate its hegemony over East Asia after the collapse of the Soviet Union. However, one year later, these critics agreed that the time was appropriate for a more positive consideration of the concept. No doubt the North Korean announcement of its intended withdrawal from the NPT regime that also occurred in March 1992 (one week after this change in attitude) played some role.

Subsequently, from January to March 1995, a panel of five senior specialists in Asian security issues from China, Russia, the Republic of Korea, Japan, and the United States met in Atlanta to consider a limited nuclear-free zone (LNFZ) for Northeast Asia under the sponsorship of the Center for International Strategy, Technology, and Policy at the Georgia Institute of Technology. The PRC permitted a senior scholar of the China Institute for Contemporary Foreign Relations to participate. Further, five distinguished Chinese (retired general, retired diplomat, nuclear expert, academic specialist, and a businessman) participated in meetings during 1996 in Buenos Aires, Argentina, and Bordeaux, France, where an expanded senior panel of twenty-five specialists from the same five countries considered a draft concept paper. The Bordeaux meeting decided to establish an international secretariat in Atlanta to arrange further discussions designed to generate governmental interest in the LNFZ in the five countries.

The above activity guarantees nothing, but it is clear that some Chinese at an "unofficial" level are very willing to engage in a dialogue that focuses on the specifics of a LNFZ that is restricted and is seen as a first step in a long-term process. It also offers some a ready answer to the accusations that there is an international plot afoot to "contain" China. This would be evidence of integration and engagement at a very important regional level. There is, however, little to indicate, at present, that such interest at the unofficial level can be extrapolated into official government interest. Our best answer to China's willingness to play in a LNFZ must be a very cloudy *maybe*.

RUSSIA: PLAYER OR NOT?

With respect to Russia, the principal question raised in discussions on the LNFZ concept is who will pay rather than who will play. Members of the National Security Council in Moscow and the security advisor to President Yeltsin expressed keen interest in the idea once the Buenos Aires meeting recommended the inclusion of Alaska in the projected zone.

Members of the Russian security community were very interested in having Vladivostok established as the agency headquarters for this sub-regional confidence-building measure; they saw it as a way to regain some specific national role in the region and realize some greater degree of integration in the political affairs of the area.

JAPAN: A CHANCE TO LEAD

Elections in Japan during 1995 and 1996 have produced a growing consensus in Japan on security issues among dominant leadership groups. Equally important, the role of the Self-Defense Forces (SDF) in the Kobe earthquake of February 1995 has improved the image of the SDF, which is now considered constitutional and recognized as an instrument needed by the government to fulfill its responsibilities. As a result of this change in climate, the security debate reaches into more substantive arenas. Such issues as peacekeeping operations roles, restructuring of the SDF, redeployment of American forces from Okinawa to other Japanese islands, and appropriate CBMs for the future can be addressed.

With the security policy community within the Ministry of Foreign Affairs and the Defense Agency taking measures to reorganize and take a better look at such ideas, especially multilateral initiatives, the bureaucratic groundwork is being created for a more creative role for Japan in international security issues.

The announcement by France of a series of nuclear tests in the South Pacific and China's two tests since the extension of the NPT raised proliferation awareness to new heights as the 50th anniversary of the use of nuclear weapons in World War II was observed. The announcement by President Lee Teng-Hui of Taiwan of the need to re-examine the Republic of China's nuclear-weapons option in light of the bombast and sword-rattling military exercises of the People's Republic of China added to the negative environment. However, the announcement by the U.S. president of American intentions to support zero-level testing of nuclear weapons, as well as the announcement that the United States would now welcome a nuclear-free zone for Southeast Asia clearly indicated that the United States was moving forward in the face of strong military counsel against such moves.

In this environment, in early August 1995, the Japanese Diet passed a strong condemnation of both France and China in a unanimous action. A four-paragraph anti-nuclear resolution demonstrated that this is an area where leadership is possible.[1]

Japan can act to support a LNFZ only if a significant consensus exists between the bureaucratic players and the political parties. Significant action by one of the parties—the Social Democratic Party of Japan (SDPJ), for example—would seem appropriate given the need for a new platform that continues to demonstrate their interest in nonproliferation but that also reveals a continuation of a new pragmatism. At this point, however, there is no clear indication of a Japanese initiative in this area.

A U.S. SIGNAL NEEDED

Recent U.S. moves related to the Comprehensive Test Ban Treaty (CTBT) augur well for a favorable U.S. approach in the future to the Northeast Asia LNFZ proposal. Initially, the United States justified inaction on the proposal by arguing that early drafts of the projected treaty establishing the zone did not envisage the United States as a participating party. The U.S. reaction, in that context, was that the initiative for the zone should come from Asia. As already indicated, however, the deliberations of the Senior Panel from January to March 1995 resulted in recommendation that a portion of U.S. territory, Alaska, should be included within the zone. This makes it incumbent upon the United States to examine the concept positively at this stage and send a signal—only a signal—to the governments of East Asia. Once the United States indicates a positive attitude toward the concept, support for the LNFZ from East Asian governments, with the possible exception of North Korea, will begin to coalesce, at least initially.

The realization of an LNFZ in Northeast Asia will not be accomplished overnight, but given our experience with the test ban and the Latin American nuclear-free zone, having something ready when policy is finally changed affords the opportunity for rapid success.

Note

[1] *The Japan Times*, August 4, 1995, p. 1.

DENUCLEARIZATION INITIATIVES: WILL THE 'BIG BOYS' PLAY?

TAKEHIKO KAMO

Fifty years after the first explosion of nuclear weapons is "a timely juncture to take stock of what 'the bomb' has meant to the state."[1] The fact is, however, that even after the end of the Cold War, we are still living in the nuclear age. Unless nuclear weapons are eliminated or fully controlled by an international organization, there will always be the risk of nuclear war.

The United States has played a consistent and coherent role in nuclear disarmament and arms control since the end of the Cold War. However, U.S.–Russian nuclear disarmament and arms control processes have not accelerated since the late 1980s as much as we had expected, although START I did finally enter into force at the end of December 1994. As the *Strategic Survey 1994-95* put it, "in the intervening years, the problem quadrupled. In three years, the US had to find the magic formula to ensure that Belarus, Kazakhstan and Ukraine, which acquired nuclear weapons on their territories when the Soviet Union ruptured, would voluntarily surrender them."[2]

I agree with Robert S. McNamara's belief that, even though substantial reductions in nuclear forces may be attempted by START II, the danger of nuclear war will have been lowered but not eliminated.[3] Considering the importance of denuclearization in the post–Cold War era, it is imperative that both the United States and Russia make every possible effort to promote nuclear disarmament and arms control on a bilateral basis. The next step after the achievement of START II goals in the year 2003 will be of decisive importance.

To control the proliferation of nuclear weapons and accelerate the denuclearization process at the global level, both the United States and Russia must make clear the objectives for the final stage of arms control and disarmament in the START framework, no matter how difficult this might be. The next step after START II is not clear to the international community; Presidents Clinton and Yeltsin therefore need to talk about the next phase beyond START II.

LACK OF CONCRETE PROGRESS IN DENUCLEARIZATION

Neither the U.S.-Russian disarmament efforts with respect to nuclear forces nor the multilateral denuclearization efforts among the nuclear states (the five permanent members of the United Nations Security Council) have been successful in the 1990s. The United States has taken the lead in efforts to find a large majority in favor of the indefinite and unconditional extension of the NPT. As the *Strategic Survey* predicted, "No world body of this size (the 171 signatories), dealing with a subject of this complexity, could be expected to show much consensus."[4] Yet the NPT was finally accepted by the United Nations General Assembly as an indefinitely and unconditionally extended treaty. In the final analysis, I agree with the extension of the NPT—simply because no other non-proliferation regime can be found at present.

The NPT extension should be welcomed by the nuclear states because it will help to prevent countries from developing nuclear weapons—a positive step to stop further nuclear proliferation. But this does not mean that the present nuclear states necessarily would be willing to take new initiatives for denuclearization processes in different regions of the world, for example in the Middle East and East Asia. The NPT regime is quite inadequate when we consider the failure of the existing nuclear-weapon states to date to take denuclearization initiatives sufficient to fulfill their pledge in Article VI of the NPT to phase out their nuclear weapons.

My view is that while the NPT should be maintained to stop nuclear proliferation, it is inadequate for achieving denuclearization or effective arms control and disarmament of nuclear forces through the multilateral efforts of the nuclear states. Because the NPT has not yet provided any concrete measures for denuclearization, either through the nuclear states or on a multilateral basis, the NPT regime is critically flawed. What is clearly missing is a multilateral framework for the five nuclear-declared states. In this context, the 1995 French official announcement of the resumption of nuclear tests in the South Pacific was deplorable. China's decision to explode a nuclear bomb is also lamentable. Both are a clear indication that "anti-denuclearization" processes are occurring just after the indefinite and unconditional extension of the NPT.

JAPAN'S POLICY ON NUCLEAR WEAPONS

Japan correctly protested the French nuclear tests through the adoption of a resolution in the Diet and through action at the United Nations in cooperation with other nations in the Asia-Pacific region. Significantly, it was not in a position to take punitive measures, such as a boycott of French imports, because that might have only exposed inconsistencies in Japan's approach toward nuclear weapons. Despite its three-part non-nuclear policy—not possessing, introducing, or producing nuclear

141

weapons—Japan depends on the nuclear umbrella of the United States. Since the end of the Cold War, the Japanese government has not clearly thought through how long and under what conditions Japan could and should depend on the U.S. "extended deterrence" policy.[5]

As for China's nuclear tests, Japan should register its protest unequivocally. It is urgent that China join with other Asian nations in a multilateral framework for negotiations on arms control and disarmament with respect to conventional weapons. In addition, multilateral confidence-building measures should be established in the Asia-Pacific region. China is increasingly important not only to Japan, but to all the Asia-Pacific nations, simply because it has not made clear its strategic direction in the 21st century, except, of course, for its great-power orientation. The recent Chinese policy of threatening Taiwan is dangerous. But, without China, no multilateral framework for nuclear arms control and disarmament will be useful or effective in this region.

PROPOSALS FOR DENUCLEARIZATION

First, I propose that both the United States and Russia urge China to join in a multilateral negotiations framework for nuclear arms control and disarmament before the end of this century. Without China's participation, the denuclearization initiatives will not be successful among the big nuclear powers.

Second, the denuclearization of East Asia (the Korean Peninsula and Japan) remains important for the prevention of nuclear proliferation. The suspected North Korean nuclear development must be stopped through U.S.–North Korea negotiations. Pyongyang should make clearer its determination not to develop nuclear bombs under any circumstances. I believe what the United States is doing through its efforts to prevent Pyongyang from acquiring nuclear weapons is basically correct. The United States has promised to supply two modern lightwater reactors to North Korea to replace the reactor it shut down to ensure that it would not produce plutonium. Japan should continue to support America's hard, but often flexible, policy to stop nuclear proliferation in East Asia. To achieve denuclearization in East Asia, the two Korean governments and Japan should start negotiations as soon as possible to achieve an international accord on this issue.

A nuclear-free zone is clearly needed on the Korean Peninsula. The danger of nuclear proliferation on the Korean Peninsula is a more immediate and urgent issue for Japan's national security than the Chinese military buildup. The underlying assumption is that Japanese society may be much more affected in psychological terms by the Korean possession of nuclear arms. The so-called "pacifism" observed in Article

9 of the Japanese Constitution may not work as favorably as we would expect if nuclear proliferation does occur on the Korean Peninsula.

Notes

[1] Daniel Deudney, "Nuclear Weapons and the Waning of the Real-State," *Daedlus*, Spring 1995, p. 209.

[2] *Strategic Survey 1994-95* (London: The International Institute for Strategic Studies, May 1995), p. 12.

[3] Robert S. McNamara, "A Long-Russia Policy for Nuclear Forces of the Nuclear Powers," paper submitted to the U.S.–Japan Study Group on Non-Proliferation and Arms Control After the Cold War, Carnegie Endowment for International Peace, Washington, D.C., June 17-19, p. 1.

[4] *Strategic Survey 1994-95, op cit.,* p. 13.

IV.
THE
NON-
PROLIFERATION
REGIME

WORKING GROUP IV

Co-Chairmen
Christopher E. Paine and Mitsuru Kurosawa

James E. Leonard
Yuzo Murayama
Leonard S. Spector
Yasuhide Yamanouchi

THE NON-PROLIFERATION REGIME

REPORT OF WORKING GROUP IV

The participants agreed that five steps are needed to sustain continuing broad support for the nuclear non-proliferation regime in the years ahead: a Comprehensive Test Ban Treaty (CTBT); a treaty prohibiting the production of fissile material for weapons; further bilateral nuclear-weapon reductions in START III, leading to the establishment of a multilateral regime for the further reduction and eventual elimination of nuclear-weapon stockpiles; stronger negative security assurances; and additional nuclear-weapons-free zones.

A FISSILE MATERIAL CUTOFF

While the CTBT negotiations are entering their final phase, with the objective of presenting a completed treaty to the United Nations General Assembly in the fall of 1996, the same may not be said of the fissile material cutoff. Even assuming that procedural obstacles are overcome and formal negotiations actually begin in Geneva, the current outlook is for a prolonged stalemate on this issue. Given this prospect, the working group felt that serious consideration should be given to partial unilateral steps that would contribute to confidence building in unstable regions and swiftly bring about a global *de facto* shutdown in the production of fissile material for weapons purposes. In some instances, pending the introduction of more extensive verification measures, national technical means of verification may serve to provide assurance that a given facility is no longer in operation.

Given the likely limitation of the cutoff to future production for weapons purposes, the group noted the need for a time-bound commitment to bring existing stocks of fissile materials under safeguards, through an arrangement comparable to Article Six of the Nuclear Non-Proliferation Treaty (NPT), which commits the nuclear-weapon states to reduce and eliminate existing nuclear weapons.

NUCLEAR-WEAPONS REDUCTIONS

The group agreed that deep START III reductions in U.S. and Russian nuclear arsenals are a necessary precondition for participation by all nuclear weapon states in a multilateral nuclear-weapons reduction regime leading toward the eventual elimination of nuclear weapons.

147

THE SAFEGUARDS REGIME

The working group likewise agreed that further measures are needed to strengthen International Atomic Energy Agency (IAEA) safeguards, including: the Agency's proposed "93 +2 Program" [1] for achieving increased transparency of nuclear programs and broader access to nuclear-related locations and sites; a more defined set of agreed procedures for implementing the IAEA's prerogative to conduct special inspections; and an extension of the safeguards regime to sensitive nuclear fuel-cycle facilities in nuclear-weapon states.

This extension could begin with bilateral data exchanges and where necessary, additional technical and financial assistance to bring about rapid improvements in national systems of nuclear-material accounting and protection that are now far below current IAEA standards. The United States and Japan, and other nations in a position to offer assistance, should increase their level of cooperation in rapidly improving the level of security and nuclear-material accounting in Russia and the other states of the former Soviet Union.

Regarding the current and future safeguards activities of the IAEA, the group agreed that reducing the secrecy surrounding safeguards inspection reports on individual countries and facilities would improve the IAEA's operations and increase international confidence in the non-proliferation regime.

Proliferation threats have evolved with the changing economic and political situation in the world, and the threat of a theft or diversion of nuclear-weapons material can emanate just as easily from within the borders of a nuclear-weapon state. The group agreed that fissile material stocks outside of, or removed from weapons, and sensitive nuclear fuel-cycle facilities in such states should no longer be excluded from coverage under the international safeguards system. The group noted the disproportion between the levels of safeguards expenditure and capability for planned reprocessing facilities in Japan and operating facilities in Russia that currently face far more credible threats of theft and diversion. This is not an argument for paying less attention to safeguarding nuclear fuel-cycle facilities in Japan, but rather for more attention to standards of security, nuclear materials accounting, and international accountability for such facilities wherever they are located.

NUCLEAR-WEAPONS-FREE ZONES

Members of the working group agreed that regional nuclear-weapons-free zones, such as those now existing for Latin America and the South Pacific and in the process of formation for Africa and Southeast Asia, are an important complement to the NPT regime.

148

Within the political context established by such zones, bilateral or regional inspection regimes can be negotiated that go beyond what is required of parties under the NPT. Within such zones, the prohibitions on stationing and use of nuclear weapons can be established without qualification, and safeguards on the production of weapon-usable materials can be replaced by a total prohibition on reprocessing and/or enrichment within the zone, as, for example, in the case of the 1992 Korean Agreement.

The group considered two approaches to the formation of a nuclear-weapons-free zone for Northeast Asia. The first approach would exclude those territories of the nuclear weapon powers that would otherwise logically be included within the natural geographic boundaries of the zone. The second approach would seek to denuclearize the relevant territories of both Russia and China within the zone prior to establishing it—by targeting further negotiated arms reductions to the weapons located on these territories.

PLUTONIUM AND THE NON-PROLIFERATION REGIME

The working group agreed that the adoption of the closed nuclear fuel cycle by many nations would pose very serious challenges to the non-proliferation regime, particularly if a proliferation of independent national fuel cycles affords a widening circle of countries with access to the weapon-grade plutonium produced in breeder blankets. The group agreed that the Japanese plutonium program itself must be continually reviewed to take into account its repercussions on regional security and nuclear disarmament efforts. Breeder reactors should be viewed as a long-term research and development option for future energy supply, and the eventual commercial deployment of breeders should be evaluated in the light of future economic, political, and security circumstances. Japan's near-term program for commercial plutonium separation and thermal recycle should likewise be reviewed for its potential impact on other states in the region and on the wider nonproliferation regime. This program must also take into consideration the current and prospective capabilities of the international system and any potential regional frameworks to safeguard these activities with an acceptable degree of uncertainty.

EXPORT CONTROLS AND ECONOMIC LEVERAGE

The working group agreed that Japan should continue its effort to gain support for export controls among other Asian states. However, any "new COCOM" should not become the vehicle for artificial divisions between groups of advanced industrial and industrializing states, but rather an effort to build a broad community of states, including states in the developing world, with greater awareness and capabilities for controlling sensitive technologies and equipment.

Both Japan and the United States are making modest attempts to use their economic leverage, such as the ability to withhold grants and loans, to support export control norms and non-proliferation goals, and opportunities exist for greater coordination and collaboration in these efforts.

AREAS OF UNCERTAINTY AND POSSIBLE DISAGREEMENT

The Japanese members of the working group were less certain than the American members that international safeguards would ultimately fail to provide an adequate degree of assurance against the abuse of the plutonium fuel cycle for weapons purposes. They indicated a need for further analysis and discussion in this area with Japanese experts who were prepared to defend the adequacy of current and planned safeguards.

There was a similar gap in the level of certainty when it came to evaluating the economics of the plutonium fuel cycle. Coming from the increasingly competitive energy marketplace in the United States, where relatively high operating and maintenance costs are leading to the premature retirement of conventional thermal-power reactors, most of the American participants do not view the far more complex and costly plutonium fuel cycle as a likely energy resource, and they believe that this judgement is unlikely to change for many decades. While there was agreement that plutonium breeder reactors were clearly not cost-competitive now, and needed considerably more development prior to commercialization, the Japanese members were reluctant to render a similar judgement on the economics of Japan's near-term program for plutonium recycling in thermal reactors and the construction of the Rokkasho-Mura reprocessing plant.

Finally, there seemed to be differing evaluations of the weight that should be placed on *political intentions* versus *inherent technical capabilities* when evaluating whether the overall proliferation risk posed by the use of plutonium fuels is acceptable or unacceptable. The American side tended to stress the technical fuel-cycle capabilities that would endure and even expand irrespective of political arrangements, while the Japanese side tended to emphasize political intentions and the social and historical factors that would be likely to inhibit weapons proliferation.

Note

[1] Under the "93+2" Program, the IAEA would increase the transparency of all member states' nuclear programs by seeking: (1) an expanded declaration from states covering all their nuclear-related activities, both present and planned; (2) the use of environmental sampling techniques to provide additional assurance regarding the absence of undeclared nuclear activities; (3) improved management and analysis of all nuclear-related information available to the agency—using the analytical construct of a proliferation "critical path"—to highlight at an early stage any information about a state's nuclear activities that may be inconsistent with its declarations to the Agency; (4) access beyond currently designated "strategic points" in a safeguarded facility to any location on the site containing the facility; (5) access to locations which are not nuclear facilities and do not contain nuclear material, but contain other declared nuclear-related activities; and (6) prompt access to undeclared locations if the need for such access is indicated by specific information received by the Agency, or is required to implement specific technical monitoring measures.

THE NPT IN ITS NEW INCARNATION

JAMES E. LEONARD

The Nuclear Non-Proliferation Treaty (NPT) has passed the most critical test that it is ever likely to face. It has been extended not just another ten years, or even twenty-five, but indefinitely. The challenge now is how to strengthen the Treaty and the broader regime, and how to reinforce it so that it will serve us effectively in the next crisis and the one after that—whatever those crises might be.

STRENGTHENING THE NPT:
SAFEGUARDS AND EXPORT CONTROLS

Strengthening the NPT has two aspects. The first, rather narrow and specific, relates to the operation of the Treaty, the safeguards system, export controls, and the "hard cases," such as North Korea. The second, broader aspect relates to dealing with the nuclear problem as a whole rather than just with horizontal proliferation. How well we do on the broad problem of nuclear weapons will have a great deal of impact on the practical problem of preventing narrow escapes from disasters like the one in Iraq.

The problems that need to be solved in strengthening the operation of the Treaty are rather well-known, and measures to deal with them are, generally, on the current agenda. The program to strengthen safeguards, the "93+2," is moving forward in a rather satisfactory manner. Money for this program may be a problem. Some months ago, there was hope that the U.S. administration might manage to get more financial support for the International Atomic Energy Agency (IAEA) in spite of the hostile attitudes in Congress toward the United Nations generally. This now appears out of the question. The State Department is even having trouble securing the tiny sums needed to finance U.S. costs for carrying out American responsibilities under the Agreed Framework for North Korea.

Export controls are an essential complement to the NPT and its safeguards system. They were challenged at the extension conference by Iran, supported by a number of other developing countries. The industrial states that manage the export control machinery should draw the correct conclusion from what happened in New York. They should work to improve the machinery in ways that will maximize support for it in the Third World. This should *not* involve turning the machinery into a General Assembly, consensus-of-the-whole-world type of operation. It *should* involve drawing important, responsible members of the non-aligned movement into the work of export control, and it should involve increasing the transparency of this work so that it can be better defended against critics both in the North and in the South.

PLUTONIUM AND HIGHLY ENRICHED URANIUM

Plutonium remains a problem with no solution yet in sight. And now, unhappily, highly enriched uranium (HEU) is on the agenda again. A regrettable decision by Germany to go forward with an HEU reactor for research work has stirred up an issue that many believed had been put behind us. It was an HEU research reactor supplied by France to Iraq that the Israelis bombed in 1981. Moreover, the HEU in the Baghdad reactor was the key element in the "Crash Program" to build a weapon initiated by Saddam Hussein in late 1990.

But plutonium is a much larger problem than HEU. The United States was correct in not trying to use the extension conference to put pressure on Japan and other advocates of plutonium recycling to abandon their programs. That does not mean, however, that the problem has gone away. We certainly do not want plutonium accumulations in North or South Korea, Iran, Pakistan, or any other area of proliferation concern. If Japan, Russia, India, France, and perhaps a few more countries are going to go forward in defiance of all the laws of economics and invest billions of dollars in plutonium recycling, then they owe it to the rest of the world to face the proliferation consequences. We can reasonably expect new ideas, or old ideas brought up to date, on how to prevent the example that Japan and others are setting from being misused by potential proliferators. It is not adequate for Japan or Germany to argue that *they* are above suspicion. I believe that *they are* above suspicion, but many others are not. How can those others be deterred from following the Japanese and German example?

ENFORCEMENT BY THE U.N. SECURITY COUNCIL

Other problems connected to the operation of the NPT deserve study, but one of them—the problem of enforcement—is of particular importance. The Statute of the IAEA puts the responsibility for enforcement on the United Nations Security Council. That burden would be on the Council in any case, because of its U.N. Charter responsibility to deal with threats to the peace. The Council's statement at its Summit Meeting in January 1992 explicitly recognized this responsibility and promised to meet it. The opportunity came more quickly than expected when North Korea declared it was leaving the NPT.

We know what then happened. The Security Council, the United States, China, and Jimmy Carter more or less dealt with the crisis. We were lucky. The Council as an institution had no background, no ideas, and no procedures at hand for managing this sort of development. Things are not in any way better or different today.

A study group organized by the United Nations Association of the USA (UNA-USA) has proposed some modest measures that could better prepare the Security Council to face its responsibilities the next time. The Council could, for example, make it clear that there does not have to be a treaty violation to move it into action. It can act whenever it believes there is a threat to the peace, whether a treaty has been violated or not. It might prevent a crisis from arising if this fact were widely understood and accepted. Another step the Security Council could take would be to equip itself with a small, expert staff that could warn of problems and develop possible solutions before a situation became acute.

These suggestions by the UNA-USA have been discussed in New York, and it is possible that something will come of them. They are extremely modest and much more thought needs to be given to the enforcement problem.

Enlarging the Security Council might make it more effective, but it is also possible that enlargement by itself would produce a less effective institution. Japan and Germany are the two states that are widely supported to become permanent members of an enlarged Council. They would earn the gratitude of the international community if they could come forward together with a proposal for measures to ensure that a larger Council really would work in a more effective way. The problem of enforcing the norm against proliferation would be an excellent issue for Germany and Japan to use to illustrate the suggestions they might have for changes, for example, in the rules of procedure, structure, or working methods of the Council to make it more capable of meeting its responsibilities at the very pinnacle of the global security system.

PROGRAM OF ACTION FOR NUCLEAR DISARMAMENT

The second half, and in many ways the larger half, of strengthening non-proliferation is mainly, but not entirely, the responsibility of the nuclear-weapon states. It involves the fulfillment by them of their obligations under Article VI of the NPT. These obligations have been acknowledged, reaffirmed, and made more specific in the program of action for nuclear disarmament proposed by South Africa at the beginning of the NPT Conference, modified under the leadership of Ambassador Dhanapala, and adopted without dissent at the conclusion of the conference as "The Principles and Objectives for Nuclear Non-Proliferation and Disarmament."

154

The significance of the program is clear. The nuclear powers secured the indefinite extension they wanted, but that extension was *not* "unconditional." Rather, it was conditioned on their acceptance of the obligation to follow through on the program of action. That obligation is not legally binding; the NPT will not dissolve if the program is not taken seriously. But the obligation is a political and moral commitment. If it is disregarded, the nuclear powers will gravely damage their moral authority and their ability to mobilize the international community in support of a scrupulous observance of the NPT by the non-nuclear-weapon states.

BEHAVIOR OF THE NUCLEAR POWERS

The behavior of the nuclear powers in the months since the close of the conference is not encouraging. In fact, it is frightening. The Chinese test, which came before the conference documents had even been printed, was insulting. The French decision to resume testing, without any serious study of whether France needs the tests or what the tests might achieve showed a contemptuous disregard for international opinion. And then the outrageous effort in Washington to rush through the government a decision that would have converted the Comprehensive Test Ban into a more limited Threshold Test Ban came close to destroying the prospect for any kind of a test ban. The Pentagon was too greedy, and the White House rejected its push toward a threshold treaty. Both the United States and France now call for a true, zero-yield agreement. There may be a treaty to sign in 1996.

Nevertheless, we have had a narrow escape. With this sort of negative example from the nuclear powers, it is not surprising that Pakistan resumed its effort to block any progress toward a fissile-material cutoff treaty, the second item on the agreed program of action. China and the United States are the only countries with any real influence on Pakistan; and if they lightly disregard their promises, why should Pakistan take seriously its own repeated calls for the negotiation of a cutoff treaty?

It would be good to report that, despite these problems in multilateral arms control, the two major powers are moving forward on bilateral nuclear disarmament. Unhappily, for the most part, the reverse is true. Although the U.S. Senate has finally ratified the Strategic Arms Reduction Treaty II (START II), the Russian Duma has not, and there is no clear prospect that the United States and Russia will carry through with any basic reappraisal of the role of nuclear weapons or give any consideration to the "no first use" concept. We will be fortunate indeed if START II becomes effective and if there is any kind of a START III negotiation. The Anti-Ballistic Missile Treaty, the very cornerstone of nuclear arms control, is also under serious attack in the U.S. Congress.

In time, of course, serious work will resume. The question is how much damage the non-proliferation regime might suffer in the meantime. No clear answer to that question can be offered at present. We can only hope that public pressure within the nuclear states and pressure on them from outside will make them faithfully fulfill of their solemn commitments.

THE NPT IN ITS NEW INCARNATION

MITSURU KUROSAWA

SIGNIFICANCE OF THE NPT CONFERENCE

The 1995 Review and Extension Conference of the Parties to the Nuclear Non-Proliferation Treaty (NPT), held in April-May 1995, was one of the most important conferences in the search for a new international security order. The conference adopted the decision, without a vote, that the NPT shall continue in force indefinitely.

The two main reasons why so many states supported the indefinite extension are: first, the United States had campaigned vigorously for the indefinite extension over the last two to three years; the Clinton Administration had given top priority to the non-proliferation issue, and high-level U.S. officials visited many countries and met with their representatives to persuade them to support the NPT indefinite extension. The second reason is that the non-aligned nations could no longer unite in support of nuclear disarmament. The disappearance of East-West confrontation made the *raison d'être* of the non-aligned movement ambiguous. These countries are now more concerned with regional security than with global security, and this divided the non-aligned states into supporters and non-supporters of the NPT indefinite extension. But the apparent progress in nuclear disarmament with the Strategic Arms Reduction Treaties (START) and the comprehensive test ban negotiations encouraged the majority of non-aligned countries to support the indefinite extension.

The decision on indefinite extension was not adopted alone, but as a political package with two important statements appended to the main conference declaration. These statements were intended to strengthen the non-proliferation regime and at the same time to proceed toward nuclear disarmament in both procedural and substantive respects.

The statement on "Strengthening the Review Process for the Treaty" stipulates that Review Conferences should continue to be held every five years, with the next in the year 2000, and that the preparatory committee should hold a meeting for ten days in each of the three years prior to the Review Conference to consider substantive matters for nuclear disarmament and make recommendations for the Review Conference.

The statement on "Principles and Objectives for Nuclear Non-Proliferation and Disarmament" sets forth a set of principles and objec-

157

tives in accordance with which nuclear non-proliferation, nuclear disarmament, and international cooperation in the peaceful uses of nuclear energy should be vigorously pursued, and progress, achievements, and shortcomings should be evaluated periodically.

These decisions represent a compromise for which the Conference President, Jayantha Dhanapala, managed to win enough support to make a vote on indefinite extension unnecessary.

MEASURES FOR NUCLEAR DISARMAMENT

The only measure that is listed in "The Principles of Nuclear Disarmament" with a time limit is the CTBT, for which completion by the Conference on Disarmament on a universal and internationally and effectively verifiable CTBT, is to be no later than 1996. Pending the entry into force of the CTBT, the nuclear-weapon states should exercise utmost restraint.

On August 11, 1995, President Clinton endorsed a permanent end to all nuclear-weapon testing, including even small-scale hydronuclear experiments. France and the United Kingdom supported this position, and Russia is also expected to support it. This support is very important for the CTBT because the controversial scope of the Treaty is now agreed upon among four of the five nuclear-weapons states. China's remaining demand for peaceful nuclear explosions should be dropped through persuasion by the other four nuclear states.

China's two 1995 nuclear tests—one on May 15, just after the NPT review and extension conference, and the other on August 17— were most regrettable. Public response has also been especially negative to the French nuclear testing, which began in September 1995 as part of a series of nuclear tests and that has now ended. The behavior of China and France is viewed as a betrayal of the non-nuclear weapons states, since "The Principles of Nuclear Disarmament" asked the nuclear-weapon states to exercise utmost restraint in testing.

"The Principles of Nuclear Disarmament" stipulates as another concrete measure the immediate commencement and early conclusion of negotiations on a non-discriminatory and universally applicable convention banning the production of fissile material for nuclear weapons and other nuclear explosives. Although the mandate to negotiate was given to the Conference on Disarmament, the scope of a treaty, especially one on how to deal with existing stockpiles in threshold countries, is not clear —as shown in many statements made at the NPT Review and Extension Conference. As a first step, a treaty to freeze the production of fissile material should be negotiated, and the scope of prohibition should be expanded later to include the elimination of existing stockpiles.

It is not certain that START II will be ratified by Russia, and implementation of the Start I faces technical and financial difficulties. There is no mention of START III in "The Principles of Nuclear Disarmament," in spite of the fact that many delegates to the NPT conference from non-nuclear weapon(s) states argued for beginning negotiations on START III. The momentum for nuclear disarmament that emerged with the end of the Cold War should be politically maintained by beginning the negotiation of START III between Russia and the United States. Once START III is concluded, it would be possible for the United Kingdom, France, and China to initiate five-power nuclear-reduction talks.

NEGATIVE SECURITY ASSURANCES AND "NO FIRST USE"

On April 6, 1995, France, Russia, the United Kingdom, and the United States made a joint statement on negative security assurances, which was substantially the same as the earlier statements made by the three Western states. The joint statement was possible because in 1993 Russia had abandoned its earlier categorical stand against the first use of nuclear weapons. In contrast to the joint statement China has reiterated a categorical position that it would not be the first to use nuclear weapons.

"The Principles of Nuclear Disarmament" state that an internationally legally binding instrument pledging "no first use" should be negotiated among the five nuclear-weapon(s) states as soon possible. As the Cold War has ended and almost all the tactical weapons of the United States and Russia have been withdrawn, the rationale for a "first use" policy seems to have lost its legitimacy and credibility. This is the time, therefore, for the United States to reexamine its doctrine on the use of nuclear weapons.

NUCLEAR-WEAPONS-FREE ZONES

The concept of nuclear-weapons-free zones (NWFZs) was thoroughly evaluated at the NPT conference. The 1967 Tlatelolco Treaty, signed by Argentina, Brazil, and Chile, has created Latin American NWFZ. An African NWFZ is also now in effect. The Rarotonga Treaty for a NWFZ in the South Pacific will be completed with the accession to the protocols by France, the United Kingdom, and the United States. Respect and support by the nuclear-weapon states is a prerequisite for such zones to be established and maintained.

Ten Southeast Asian countries concluded a treaty in 1995 that would establish an NWFZ, but the United States and China refuse to endorse it. If the 1992 Joint Declaration on Denuclearization of the

Korean Peninsula is implemented effectively between the two Korean states, the concept of a NWFZ in Northeast Asia would gain support and Japan would have to consider joining such a zone.

MEASURES TO STRENGTHEN SAFEGUARDS

At the NPT conference, support was given to a decision by the IAEA Board of Governors aimed at further strengthening the effectiveness of IAEA safeguards in accordance with a 1993 IAEA decision to achieve tighter safeguards within two years (the "93+2" Program). The new approach is based on two concepts: "broader access to information" and "increased physical access."

In the case of measures for broader access to information, the IAEA Board of Governors has already recommended: (1) early provision of design information with respect to new nuclear facilities, and (2) provision of information on export of materials usable in nuclear activities, with a view to establishing a universal reporting system on such exports.

Further steps to increase broader access to information include: (1) an expanded declaration; (2) environmental sampling; and (3) improved analysis of information. In sharp contrast to the current system of nuclear-materials accounting and control, which only requires information on nuclear material, the expanded declaration measures are intended to increase the transparency of all nuclear activities. These measures ask a country for more information about nuclear and non-nuclear facilities, past and future activities, the nuclear fuel cycle, nuclear fuel-cycle R&D activities, buildings on the site, uranium- and thorium-ore deposits and mines, and domestic manufacturers.

The analysis of environmental samples collected in the immediate environment of a nuclear site would provide an extremely powerful tool for gaining assurance on the absence of undeclared activities at and near such sites. The IAEA believes that it may implement environmental sampling at any location to which it has access.

Increased physical access includes "broad access" and "no-notice inspections." Broad access means access to locations beyond strategic points that are permitted in the current routine inspections, as well as to any location on the sites of nuclear facilities and other locations identified in the expanded declaration. This broad access would be used primarily in two ways: to confirm information identified in the expanded declaration and other information available to the IAEA.

The no-notice (meaning no *advance* notice) inspections are intended largely for inspections at nuclear facilities and would be used under complementary legal authority at other locations identified in the expanded declaration. The combination of no-notice inspections, broad access, and increased cooperation with state or regional systems of accounting and control could result in significant improvements in the cost-effectiveness of a strengthened safeguards system.

Special inspections are beyond the scope of the IAEA under the "93+2" Program, but the procedures and conditions for invoking the special inspection should be made clearer so that it could be used more routinely.

The current safeguards system applies only to non-nuclear-weapon(s) states, and it has placed some burden on them. Although it is necessary to strengthen safeguards, this would be more burdensome for the non-nuclear states. We have to take into account this imbalance of burden and ask the nuclear-weapon states to take some measures to make their nuclear activities more transparent not only with respect to peaceful uses but also military uses.

SEPARATED PLUTONIUM AND THE NON-PROLIFERATION REGIME: RISKS, SAFEGUARDS, AND REMEDIES

CHRISTOPHER E. PAINE

So long as intrinsically dangerous activities may be carried on by nations, rivalries are inevitable and fears are engendered that place so great a pressure upon a system of international enforcement by police methods that no degree of ingenuity or technical competence could possibly hope to cope with them.
—from "A Report on the International Control of Atomic Energy" (the "Acheson-Lilienthal Report"), March 16, 1946

The prospects for economic use of plutonium in the nuclear fuel cycle for the next fifty to one hundred years[1] are negligible, and the accelerating trend toward global economic and security interdependence make obsolete purely national strategies of "energy independence" via plutonium breeding and recycling. Thus the benefits of spent-fuel reprocessing for nuclear waste management hardly offset the nuclear proliferation risks that stem from the presence of separated plutonium in the nuclear fuel cycle. Despite the obvious cost penalties to electricity consumers and taxpayers, the insistence of some national governments on continuing their plutonium separation and recycling programs raises the question whether the current non-proliferation regime, based on international monitoring of autonomous national nuclear activities to ensure their peaceful use, can adequately mitigate both the immediate and longer-term proliferation risks associated with plutonium separation and use. These risks can be summarized as follows:

- **An increasing global likelihood of nuclear catastrophe.** Small quantities of weapon-grade, fuel-grade, or reactor-grade plutonium can be used to make efficient, powerful nuclear bombs as well as inefficient crude bombs and terrorist explosive devices.

- **A further diffusion of nuclear explosive material.** National separation, recycling, and breeding of plutonium on a commercial scale place an insupportable burden on the current and prospective capabilities of the IAEA safeguards system to promptly detect thefts or diversions of plutonium (Pu)-bomb quantities from peaceful use.

- **An inherent military potential for "peaceful" nuclear programs.** "Civilian" plutonium programs provide a legitimate cover for any

162

country to acquire and stockpile nuclear explosive materials. They help to sustain a global technology base in chemical separation, processing, and Pu-metallurgy that has been and will continue to be applied to clandestine military programs.

- *An increasing global potential for Nuclear Non-Proliferation Treaty (NPT) "breakout."* Nations that have "legally" acquired a stockpile of separated plutonium or separation facilities under safeguards, but then undergo political upheaval or a change in national strategy, could suddenly emerge as nations capable of building nuclear arsenals.

- *An increased danger of proliferation in the event of societal "breakdown."* Stores of separated plutonium and fresh plutonium-bearing fuel could be seized by contending political forces or sold to organized criminal elements, other governments, or sub-national groups.

- *An obstacle to deep nuclear arms reductions.* National stockpiles of separated "civilian" plutonium and operable Pu-production facilities will act as a barrier to deeper reductions and eventual elimination of nuclear weapons held by declared and undeclared nuclear-weapon states.

"CIVILIAN" PLUTONIUM: THE WEAPONS DANGER

It should be understood and frankly acknowledged by all parties to the plutonium debate that the security risks arise not only because of the possibility of ongoing small diversions of plutonium from "peaceful" programs, but also because the civilian plutonium fuel cycle itself represents an *inherent capacity* for future weapon production. Whether or not a given nation-state currently views its plutonium capacity in this light, the prevailing quasi-anarchy of the international system virtually assures that other states, and particularly their military establishments, will perceive a nuclear weapons "hedge" option in the making and will formulate their own future security plans accordingly. If nothing else, the current debate about "counter-proliferation" reveals that the U.S. national security establishment (and perhaps others) is never likely to view the NPT and its associated safeguards system as a sufficient substitute for a preemptive nuclear deterrent as well as conventional strike capabilities against "rogue states" who might use or seek coercive advantage from their arsenals of mass destruction.

More and better safeguards on plutonium use will not by themselves alleviate this political and strategic problem. In fact, by possibly encouraging development of additional plutonium fuel-cycle facilities under essentially national control, improved IAEA safeguards for sensitive fuel-cycle facilities could accentuate the conflict between visions of a future "plutonium economy" and current nuclear disarmament efforts. Over the long term, a possible escape from this dilemma lies down one of the following pathways:

1. Complete internationalization of sensitive fuel-cycle facilities under U.N. Security Council auspices, along the lines originally envisioned by the Acheson-Lilienthal Plan;

2. An international convention banning plutonium separation (or isotopic enrichment beyond 20 percent U-235) *per se*; or

3. Banning these activities when conducted by private commercial entities or agencies of national governments, thereby leaving the door open to proposals for genuine international ownership and control of fuel-cycle facilities, should a real economic need arise in the future.

In the meantime, nations having or planning civilian nuclear energy programs with closed fuel cycles could make an important contribution to the nuclear disarmament process by voluntarily deferring further separation of plutonium until at least the following three conditions are met: (1) The existing global inventories of separated plutonium, including military stocks, are radically reduced; (2) Effective international institutions and technical controls are in place that will permit civilian plutonium use without adding significantly to the risk of nuclear-weapon proliferation; and (3) Use of plutonium in the nuclear fuel cycle represents an economically rational investment of scarce public and private capital for energy development in free and open competition with other energy resources.

At the dawn of the nuclear age, the authors of the famous Acheson-Lilienthal Plan for international control of atomic energy clearly recognized the inherent military potential of fissionable materials used for avowedly peaceful purposes. Indeed, they believed that no widespread use of nuclear energy for civil purposes was possible or desirable without international ownership and control of the full nuclear fuel cycle.

A MORAL AND POLITICAL LIMBO

Despite the fact that all types of plutonium (save relatively pure Pu-238) have an inherent capability to be used in small quantities as nuclear explosive materials, the NPT allows production and use of separated plutonium (and highly enriched uranium) under internationally monitored commitments of peaceful use. Fortunately, current international practice by the nuclear suppliers no longer conforms to the "right" of unhindered access claimed by some NPT non–nuclear weapons states to all aspects of nuclear energy development for peaceful purposes.[2] However, this contradictory state of affairs leaves the issue of the ultimate legitimacy of sensitive nuclear fuel-cycle facilities in a moral and political limbo that works to the long-term disadvantage of the nuclear non-proliferation regime—by fostering both the appearance and the reality of "discrimination" while delaying implementation of more effective controls.

On the one hand, if the international community deems both the short- and long-term proliferation risks posed by such facilities to be manageable, via an enhanced safeguards approach, then all such "civilian" plutonium facilities and stockpiles, in both nuclear-weapon and non-nuclear states, should be encased in a far more rigorous international safeguards regime than the one achieved so far. From a technical perspective, such an enhanced regime will still be unable to provide a high degree of assurance that small thefts or diversions, exceeding a technically valid "significant quantity," will be detected at bulk handling facilities. Nor, in most instances, will the criterion of "timely warning" of such losses be satisfied.

By denying the ongoing "dual-use" of safeguarded facilities for weapons production, the current safeguards system plays an important and useful role. But this role by itself is insufficient to protect international security from proliferation threats in the years ahead. In a future "plutonium economy" with massive flows of fissionable material, the challenge to improved IAEA safeguards would not be detecting discrete large-scale diversions of material, but rather numerous small leaks in the system that the agency would be powerless to prevent, leading to a flourishing black market in nuclear explosive materials. Overshadowing these day-to-day risks would be the ever present prospect of a rapid chain reaction "breakout" from the NPT under the stress of geopolitical conflicts far beyond the control of the IAEA.

"BREAKOUT" AND "BREAKDOWN"

The world must consider not only the possibility of treaty "breakout" but also that of societal "breakdown," in which vast stores of separated plutonium could be subject to seizure by contending political or ethnic factions, or to insider theft and sale to organized criminal elements, other governments, and sub-national groups. The dangerous vulnerability and repeated thefts of fissile material in Russia today is a harbinger of what we might expect to occur in a future plutonium economy, particularly if the present pattern of national programs and weak international controls is extended to cover extensive commercial repro-cessing and the deployment of breeders. A well-designed non-proliferation regime should actively take account of and seek to mini-mize these risks, or at least do nothing that would contribute to them.

On the other hand, if the international community deems the inherent proliferation risks of civilian plutonium use to be, as suggested by this paper, unacceptable *even with an enhanced safeguards regime*, then the prevailing interpretation of rights and obligations regarding safe-guarded transfers of nuclear technology for peaceful purposes (under Article IV of the NPT) should be changed to bar all transfers involving sensitive fuel-cycle activities. This revised interpretation would view any such transfers as violating Article I's injunction: "*not in any way to assist* . . . any non–nuclear weapon state to... acquire nuclear weapons or other nuclear explosive devices," and of undermining Article II's obligation on non-nuclear states "not to seek any assistance in the man-ufacture" of nuclear explosive devices.

This shift in emphasis is not as big a step as it might seem at first, given the prevailing, if not universal, restrictive norms for overt nuclear commerce already being observed in parallel with the NPT, and given Article IV's own requirement that the use of nuclear energy for peace-ful purposes be undertaken "without discrimination and *in conformity with Articles I and II of this Treaty.*" To meet the non-discrimination cri-terion, such a revised interpretation of the NPT would require the ter-mination or indefinite deferral of plutonium separation programs in *all states*, not merely in those states of current proliferation concern, and the application of safeguards to all separated plutonium existing outside of, or removed from, the arsenals of the nuclear-weapon states.

An intermediate approach would adopt the revised NPT inter-pretation outlined above as it applies to independent national or joint multinational activities, but it would not foreclose the prospect that the plutonium fuel cycle might eventually be pursued on a truly interna-tionalized basis, if and when a genuine economic need arises, under the direct supervision of the U.N. Security Council—much as J. Robert Oppenheimer originally envisioned almost fifty years ago.

Notes

[1] A 1993 analysis conservatively estimated that at or below $220/kg—$130 less than the "break-even price" for introducing MOX fuels—it would be profitable to extract 8 million tons of uranium yellowcake worldwide. At 4,400 tons per GWe plant lifetime, that is enough uranium to fuel 1,800 reactors—five time the world's current installed capacity—for thirty years, or to fuel the current capac-

ity for 150 years! See B.G. Chow and K.A. Solomon, "Limiting the Spread of Weapon-Usable Fissile Materials," RAND National Defense Research Institute, Santa Monica, CA 1993, pp. 36-38.

[2] In the 1970s, a number of countries, including Pakistan, Argentina, Brazil, South Korea, and Taiwan, sought access to reprocessing technology, ostensibly for peaceful purposes. The historical record shows that each one of these countries also had a secret nuclear-weapon development program.

SEPARATED PLUTONIUM AND THE NON-PROLIFERATION REGIME: RISKS, SAFEGUARDS, AND REMEDIES

YASUHIDE YAMANOUCHI

Since the breakup of the Soviet Union in 1991, the newly independent states of the former Soviet Union have been trying to develop market economies, increase cooperation within the Commonwealth of Independent States (CIS), and establish stable domestic governance.

Information about nuclear programs in the former Soviet Union has increasingly become available to other governments. The task of denuclearization in the CIS countries is unique and complex. Disarmament, military-to-industry conversion, and dealing with environmental problems are inseparable tasks toward which Moscow, municipal governments, and supportive outside governments are working, but not always in a coordinated manner.

This paper discusses the size and scope of the bilateral nuclear safety and denuclearization programs of Japan and the CIS countries, together with some of the current problems and a future agenda.

The program activities of the Japanese government fall into three categories (see Table 1):

- Assistance for nuclear operations safety;

- Support for introduction of the State System of Accounting for the Control of Nuclear Materials; and

- Financial assistance for the construction of denuclearization facilities.

Two Japanese ministries and one agency are responsible for these activities—the Ministry of International Trade and Industry (MITI), the Ministry of Foreign Affairs (MFA), and the Science and Technology Agency (STA).

The Freedom Support Act and the Cooperative Threat Reduction (Nunn-Lugar) Program provided the legal framework for similar U.S. program activities. A loose oversight mechanism works through the National Security Council, chaired by a senior official of the Department of State. In Japan, on the other hand, until now no coordinating mechanism exists to carry out the Japanese programs; officials share information informally at small meetings.

168

TABLE 1

PROJECT	PURPOSE	BUDGET/YEAR /MINISTRY
Support for accident detection system in Leningrad nuclear power plant	Introduction of detection system for leaks from cooling pipes during plant operation of Soviet-type nuclear reactors	¥5.01 billion 1993-95 STA
International nuclear operation safety training	Training for nuclear operators and specialists from CIS and Eastern European countries	¥680 million 1993-95 STA
Consultative delegations	Sending of delegations of Japanese nuclear specialists to former Soviet Union and Eastern Europe for consultations on nuclear safety	¥380 million 1993-95 STA
Support through IAEA program activities	Participation of Japanese specialists and funding of IAEA safety evaluation project of Soviet-type nuclear-power plants	¥700 million 1992-95 STA, MITI, MFA
Support through OECD* nuclear organization program activities	Long-term support for improvement of nuclear facilities in CIS and Eastern European countries	¥100 million 1993-95 STA
Technical support to Slovakia	Study on the safe disposal of Slovakian A1 research reactor	¥50 million 1995 STA
International workshop/training for nuclear plant operation safety	Training for 100 operators/year from CIS and Eastern European countries for ten years	¥5.26 billion 1992-95 MITI
Contribution to international programs for the support of nuclear safety	Financial support for multilateral support mechanism	¥1.89 billion MFA 1992-94
Construction of training center at Novovoronezh power plant	Introduction of a nuclear reactor stimulator for operator training	¥3.89 billion MITI 1993-95

• Organisation for Economic Co-operation and Development.

169

PROGRAM FOR NUCLEAR OPERATIONS SAFETY

Japan's commitment to nuclear operation safety began in 1992, when MITI and the Russian Ministry of Atomic Energy agreed on the construction of a nuclear power plant operation training center at the Novovoronezh nuclear complex. MITI is conducting seminars and on-the-job training each year for some 100 nuclear operators from the CIS and East European countries. This project, which began in 1993, is to continue for ten years. The STA's three-year project to introduce an accident-detection system in the Leningrad Nuclear Power Plant was also started in 1993. The STA is holding seminars and providing training for personnel at its own facilities. The STA, MITI, and MFA are cooperating to provide support for multilateral programs, such as financing for the 1992 IAEA evaluation of older types of Soviet power reactors.

The total budgetary funding authorized through July 1995 is ¥12.16 billion. Table 1 lists the projects, their purpose, and the ministry or agency responsible for the projects.

DENUCLEARIZATION PROGRAMS

The Japanese government has concluded framework agreements to establish bilateral committees with Russia, Kazakhstan, Belarus, and Ukraine. The MFA is responsible for five projects under the denuclearization program activities. In April 1993, Japan pledged ¥11.7 billion (about $100 million) for these activities, of which 70 percent is for Russia, 15 percent for Ukraine, 10 percent for Kazakhstan, and 5 percent for Belarus. Japan also pledged ¥20 million to fund the International Science and Technology Center in Moscow.

Kazakhstan, Belarus, and Ukraine became new non–nuclear weapons states following the conclusion of the Lisbon Protocol in mid-1992. Japan began bilateral meetings with these countries in 1993 to assist them to establish their SSACs and to facilitate IAEA inspections. The MFA's Science and Nuclear Energy Division is responsible for these activities in collaboration with the STA and other Japanese organizations that are under STA's mandate. Japan's Power Reactor and Nuclear Fuel Development Corporation has provided material accountancy facilities to the Kazakhstan Aktau nuclear complex for its NB350 reactor (sodium-cooled, fast-breeder reactor, fueled by highly enriched uranium or plutonium). The corporation operates Japan's fast-breeder reactors and has the accountancy know-how for these types of reactors. The Nuclear Research Center has assisted Belarus research institutions in several areas, including record and reporting systems.

Ukraine may receive assistance once bilateral consultative meetings have produced a framework agreement, and Lithuania is another likely future candidate for assistance.

The following three programs for the Russian Federation are the responsibility of the MFA's Arms Control and Disarmament Division. In cooperation with the U.S. Nunn-Lugar Program, the Japanese government will be providing funds for the construction of fissile materials storage in the Mayak highly enriched uranium and plutonium depository, once the construction plans are completed.

In cooperation with the United States, the Japanese government is providing funds for the purchase of commodities needed to transport nuclear materials; these include civilian goods such as portable wireless and video equipment, and specialty items such as U.S.–made armored blankets and protection suits.

Japan's pledge to fund the construction of disposal facilities for the submarine-launched ballistic-missile liquid fuel has not yet been fulfilled. Although it is reported that the Russians have the technology to dispose of the poisonous liquid fuel, they have not yet decided where to locate such facilities.

Several factors prompted the Japanese government's 1993 pledge of assistance for denuclearization in the former Soviet Union—a major reason being the Russian Navy's nuclear waste dumping in the Sea of Japan.

The most important of these was evidence of continuous, large-scale nuclear waste dumping by the Soviet/Russian Navy and the Ministry of Transportation since the mid-1960s. According to one account, the Russians dumped nuclear wastes six times into the Sea of Japan in 1992 alone. The report also confirmed an accidental small nuclear explosion in August 1985, resulting from improper treatment of a submarine reactor during fuel exchange at the Russian Pacific Fleet harbor near Vladivostok.

During the October 1993 visit of Russian President Yeltsin to Japan, the two governments concluded the Japan–Russia Cooperation Agreement for the Disposal of Nuclear Weapons. Despite the agreement, the Russian Navy shortly thereafter dumped into the Sea of Japan 900 tons of additional low-level liquid nuclear waste that reportedly originated from the cooling water of nuclear submarine reactors. The Russian Navy has stopped further dumping, but Russian officials have stated that, since Russia's present nuclear storage capacity for its low-level wastes is inadequate, ocean dumping would have to resume in the future.

The Japanese government is offering an international tender for a nuclear waste processing facility that will probably be located on a floating barge near Vladivostok. Although the tendering process is prolonged, it is expected that the successful bidder will enable the Primorskiy Krai municipal government to handle radioactive liquid wastes at such a facility in the near future.

PROBLEMS AND FUTURE AGENDA

Because of its status as a non-nuclear-weapon state, Japan's capacity to provide assistance for denuclearization is limited. Japan also intentionally refrains from dealing with sensitive areas such as the dismantling of nuclear weapons. Instead it uses its comparative advantage in special areas, such as the improvement of nuclear operations safety.

Japan lacks adequate human resources in the area of denuclearization. Although government officials from different ministries/agency are working together and have built up cooperative relationships through personal networks, the creation of a special branch or a task force would be desirable in view of the amount of work to be done in denuclearization.

Critics have stated that providing support for nuclear waste disposal facilities could offer the Russian Pacific Fleet an opportunity to increase its nuclear submarine operations. While this might result in the short run, considering the number of vessels that will disposed of through the Strategic Arms Reduction Treaty (START) process, support for the Russian Navy's decommissioning will bring significant benefits. Putting denuclearization of the countries of the former Soviet Union in the perspective of arms control and disarmament is important. More assistance for the dismantling of their naval vessels can be part of the future agenda.

EXPORT CONTROLS:
IS HARDWARE THE KEY TODAY?

LEONARD S. SPECTOR

Although the diffusion of advanced scientific and industrial capabilities has brought the development of weapons of mass destruction and advanced delivery systems within the grasp of an increasing number of regional powers, it is self-evident that controlling transfers of hardware needed for the manufacture of such arms remains an important element in international efforts to retard the spread of weapons of mass destruction and advanced delivery systems. Imported hardware and technology remain a significant factor in the efforts of states such as Iran, Libya, Iraq, and Pakistan to develop nuclear, chemical, and biological weapons, as well as missile delivery systems.[1]

Moreover, the fact that virtually all of the advanced industrialized states, as well as a growing number of industrializing nations, support international regimes to restrict exports of hardware and technology relevant to the production and use of such armaments is testimony to the widely shared view that such exports are an appropriate source of international concern.

THE JAPANESE ROLE

As detailed previously,[2] Japan has been an active participant in the key multilateral non-proliferation export control regimes—the Nuclear Suppliers Group, the Missile Technology Control Regime (MTCR), the Australia Group, and the recently initiated "Wassenaar Arrangement." Japan has not, however, embraced an important element of U.S. activism in enforcing the first three of these regimes. While the United States has adopted legislation that imposes economic sanctions against persons outside the United States who violate international standards of behavior by trafficking in the commodities these regimes regulate, Japan is not known to have adopted parallel legislation[3] and thus is not acting as aggressively as the United States to police international export control norms.

THE AMERICAN ROLE

Since 1991, the United States has adopted three major laws to enforce export controls internationally through the imposition of economic sanctions:

- The provisions of the 1991 Defense Authorization Act, imposing sanctions on foreign persons who knowingly violate, as either buyers or sellers, the guidelines of the MTCR;

- The provisions of the Chemical and Biological Weapons Control and Warfare Elimination Act of 1991, imposing sanctions on persons who knowingly export, from any country, goods of a type regulated by U.S. law and who thereby contribute to the efforts of a foreign country or entity to use or acquire chemical or biological weapons (CBWs); and

- The provisions of the Nuclear Proliferation Prevention Act of 1994 (NPPA), imposing sanctions on persons who knowingly and materially contribute, through the export of goods from any country, to the efforts of any group or non-nuclear-weapon state to acquire unsafeguarded special nuclear material or to use or acquire any nuclear explosive device. This law also imposes sanctions against any country that "aids or abets" any non-nuclear-weapon state to acquire unsafeguarded special nuclear material or a nuclear explosive device.[4]

In addition, U.S. laws adopted in the late 1970s, which were updated in the 1994 NPPA, require the termination of U.S. economic and military aid to: (1) any state that exports uranium enrichment or plutonium separation equipment to a non-nuclear-weapon state, unless all nuclear materials and facilities in the importing country are placed under International Atomic Energy Agency inspection; (2) any non-nuclear-weapon state that imports uranium enrichment or plutonium separation equipment unless all of its nuclear materials and facilities are placed under International Atomic Energy Agency inspection; (3) any state that transfers a nuclear device, or related components or design information, to a non-nuclear-weapon state; and (4) any non-nuclear-weapon state that receives or detonates a nuclear explosive device or that receives related components or design information.

The laws in these three areas of export control are structured along generally parallel lines.[5] Sanctions in each case are triggered by a determination by the U.S. president that an export has violated the particular law at issue. For the laws dealing with missile and CBW-related exports, sanctions must then be imposed for a mandatory two-year (missile) or one-year (CBW) period, after which the president may waive the continuation of sanctions if he determines this to be in the national interest of the United States, a standard that can be easily met. The laws penalizing improper nuclear exports generally permit the president to waive sanctions immediately, but the standards that must be met before the waivers can be exercised vary, and in some cases they are so strict that the waiver becomes virtually unusable.[6]

The content of the sanctions for these different categories of exports also varies widely:

- Under the law penalizing missile-related exports, the severity of sanctions is linked to the importance of the regime violation involved. The most serious infractions trigger a total ban on U.S. exports to the buyer and seller and a total ban on U.S. government contracts with the buyer and seller; in addition the president has the discretion to ban imports from the buyer and seller. Lesser infractions trigger a ban on missile-related U.S. exports to the buyer and seller, and a ban on U.S. government contracts related to these areas.[7]

- Under the law penalizing CBW-related exports, the sanctions are a ban on the seller entity's receiving any U.S. government procurement contracts and a ban on the seller entity's importing any product into the United States.

- Under the law penalizing improper nuclear exports, the sanction for persons whose exports contribute to the production of special nuclear material is limited to a ban on the seller entity's receiving any U.S. government procurement contracts; the sanction imposed against countries for "aiding or abetting" any state to acquire a nuclear explosive device or unsafeguarded nuclear materials is a ban on U.S. Export-Import Bank financing of any exports to that country; and the sanction for transfering enrichment, plutonium-separation technology, or nuclear explosive devices or their components is the termination of U.S. economic and military aid to both the seller and buyer states.

To date, the United States has imposed sanctions in all three sensitive export areas. The table at the end of this chapter lists the episodes involved. As of March 1996, the Clinton Administration was also considering the imposition of sanctions under the "aiding and abetting" provisions of the NPPA for the first time.[8]

THE IMPORTANCE OF SANCTIONS

To be sure, the imposition of sanctions in these instances has not always led the target of the sanctions to cease its offending behavior. Overall, however, the use of sanctions—and the threat to use them—has been a valuable tool in enhancing international adherence to international export-control norms.

First, in some cases, ongoing transfers violating of a particular export control norm have in fact been halted, as in Russia's 1993 decision to eliminate the transfer of production technology from its sale of cryogenic rocket engines to India.

Second, in cases where a particular transaction has continued even after the United States has imposed sanctions, the negotiations surrounding the sanctions often have led the exporting country to take steps to comply with the rules of the relevant export control regime prospectively. Russia's application for membership in the MTCR, for example, was accelerated by this process, as was China's decision to adhere to the original MTCR guidelines.

Third, the threat of sanctions appears to have been an effective tool in itself, contributing, for example, to China's decision not to export complete M-9 missiles to any country and not to export M-11 missiles to Iran and Syria. U.S. officials have stated that the threat of sanctions has also been used to considerable effect on a number of occasions in the CBW arena to deter offending exports, although the details of these cases remain classified.

Fourth, the visible enforcement of MTCR, CBW, and nuclear export-control rules through the imposition of sanctions has significantly reinforced the norm against proliferation in these areas by emphatically demonstrating U.S. disapproval of the behavior at issue.

Japan has yet to use economic sanctions to enforce multilateral or Japanese export-control norms outside of Japan. It has, however, announced that it is prepared to terminate or reduce economic assistance to support the goal of non-proliferation. To date, Japan has not used this tool to constrain the capabilities of emerging nuclear powers. Despite the fact that Japan is among the largest aid donors to India and Pakistan, for example, it is not known to have used this leverage to restrain the nuclear-weapon or missile programs of either state.

In mid-1995, Japan took the extraordinary step of drastically cutting economic assistance to China, slashing aid from 7.8 billion yen ($78 million) to 500 million yen ($5 million) to express disapproval of China's continued testing of nuclear weapons. This is the first publicized instance of Japan's using economic sanctions to support non-proliferation, broadly defined.[9] The wisdom of singling out China's nuclear testing for sanctions may be questioned, however. Japan is already under threat from China's nuclear-armed intermediate-range ballistic missiles, and it is not clear that the handful of tests that China is conducting before the advent of a global, Comprehensive Test Ban Treaty in 1996 will increase this threat. Most observers believe the purpose of the tests is to perfect a new nuclear warhead to be used on China's first "MIRVed" ICBM—a system that will nominally threaten the United States and Russia but not Japan.

Meanwhile, China is known to be assisting Pakistan in the construction of an unsafeguarded plutonium production reactor, has provided key components for the Pakistan's unsafeguarded Kahuta enrichment plant, and has apparently transfered M-11 components, if not complete M-11 missiles, to Pakistan—actions that could greatly increase Pakistan's nuclear-weapons potential and that will have a far greater impact on global proliferation threats than a few more Chinese nuclear tests. Yet Japan is not known to have taken any steps to penalize Beijing for these exports.

Perhaps, if the imposition of sanctions against China for its nuclear tests proves politically popular in Japan, Tokyo will be encouraged to use economic sanctions more actively in the future to support additional non-proliferation objectives.

For the moment, however, it appears that Japan is not prepared to follow U.S. activism in vigorously enforcing export-control standards internationally. This is unfortunate, because the moral, political, and economic impact of Japan's partnership with the United States on these enforcement issues could greatly strengthen international non-proliferation controls.

Notes

[1] See Leonard S. Spector, "Export Controls and Nuclear Non-Proliferation," Working Paper Prepared for the U.S.–Japan Nuclear Issues Study Group, Washington, D.C., May 5, 1995.

[2] Ibid.

[3] Based on discussions with U.S. officials and Japanese Embassy officials.

[4] In this law, "unsafeguarded" facilities refers to those that are not subject to inspection by the International Atomic Energy Agency, and the term "special nuclear material" refers to plutonium or enriched uranium. The "aiding or abetting" conduct that could trigger sanctions against countries may, but need not, involve sensitive exports.

A related provision of the 1994 Nuclear Proliferation Prevention Act imposes sanctions against any person that knowingly, materially and directly contributes *through the provision of financing* to the acquisition of unsafeguarded nuclear material or to the use, development, production, stockpiling, or other acquisition of a nuclear explosive device by an individual, group, or non-nuclear-weapon state.

[5] The laws impose sanctions on both U.S. exporters and foreign exporters (and, in some cases, on foreign importers), but since Japan undoubtedly has enacted laws that impose criminal and civil penalties against Japanese persons who violate Japanese export control laws, there is little basic difference between the U.S. and Japanese approaches in this sphere. What is missing from Japanese law are provisions that penalize violations by persons outside Japan who assist foreign missile, CBW, or nuclear programs by transfering to proliferant countries items whose export from Japan would be prohibited.

[6] The president is permitted to waive sanctions against non-nuclear-weapon states that import uranium enrichment technology but refuse to accept full-scope IAEA inspections only if he has received "reliable assurances that the state is not developing nuclear weapons" and if he determines that provision of the economic and military aid that would be prohibited if sanctions were invoked would significantly reduce the risk of proliferation by that country. In the case of Pakistan, which has been subject to this statutory provision for many years, no president has ever been able to determine that he has received the assurances necessary to waive the sanction.

[7] The law generally exempts transactions that are conducted under valid export licenses among adherents to the MTCR.

The Helms Amendment (part of the Foreign Relations Authorization Act for fiscal year 1992-93 added a provision for countries with non-market economies (principally China and North Korea) specifying that sanctions would apply not only to the government trading entities specifically involved in the transaction, but would be imposed against all government activities relating to missiles equipment and technology and to the development or production of electronics, space systems or equipment, and military aircraft.

[8] The episode at issue is China's alleged sale to Pakistan of special ring magnets intended for use in Pakistan's Kahuta enrichment facility, a facility that produces unsafeguarded special nuclear material. The sale is considered a possible violation of the provisions of the 1994 law that (1) penalize persons who make exports that contribute to the acquisition of such material and (2) that penalize countries that aid or abet others states or groups to do this. As noted in the text, the penalty against the selling entity for the prohibited export activity would be a ban on U.S. government procurement contracts to that entity; the sanction for aiding or abetting is a ban on Export-Import Bank financing for projects in China.

[9] Japan has, however, used the leverage inherent in its official development assistance to support other internationally accepted foreign policy objectives, as seen in its termination of assistance to Liberia and Sudan to support efforts to democratize these states.

Annex 1

SANCTIONS IMPOSED BY THE U.S. GOVERNMENT FOR VIOLATIONS OF U.S. LAWS PENALIZING CERTAIN EXPORT ACTIVITIES

The following is a list of known recent cases where the U.S. imposed sanctions on foreign governments, companies, and individuals who trade in chemical and biological weapons and ballistic technology.

Chemical- or Biological-Weapon (CBW) Sanctions

February 8, 1994: SPC Supachoke (Thailand), W&M Engineering (Thailand), The Handle Group (Thailand)

July 16, 1994: Nahum Manbar, Europol Holding Limited, Mana International Investment

August 19, 1994: Alberto Di Salle (Italy)

November 16, 1994: CDM Engineering SA (Switzerland), Loop SA (aka Rainstar Ltd.) (Switzerland)

November 19, 1994: Manfred Felber (Austria), Luciano Moscatelli (Australia), Gerhard Merz (Germany)

February 18, 1995: Mainway International, Asian Ways Limited, WorldCo Limited

May 18, 1995: Mainway Limited (Germany), GE Plan (Austria)

November 17, 1995: Anatoliy Kuntsevich (Russia)

Annex 2

MISSILE SANCTIONS

This list is based on information provided by Vann van Diepen, Director, Office of Weapons Proliferation Policy, U.S. Department of State, Washington, February 1996, augmented by information reported in the **Federal Register** *involving entities whose names have been withheld.*

June 25, 1991: China Great Wall Industries Group (China), China Precision Machinery Import-Export Corporation (China), Space and Upper Atmosphere Research Commission (Pakistan) [Sanctions on Chinese entities waived March 1992; sanctions expired for Pakistani entity]

September 27, 1991: Armaments Corporation of South Africa (ARM-SCOR) (South Africa) [Sanctions expired] [Note: Sanctions were also reportedly imposed at this time against certain Israeli entities, as the sellers of the technology involved, but were immediately waived when Israel agreed to apply the parameters and standards of the MTCR to future exports. See David Hoffman and R. Jeffrey Smith, "President Waives Sanctions for Israel," Washington Post, October 27, 1991.]

March 6, 1992: Glavkosmos (Russia), Indian Space Research Organization (India) [Sanctions expired]

May 6, 1992: Glavkosmos (Russia), Indian Space Research Organization (India) [Sanctions expired]

June 23, 1992: Syrian Scientific Research Center a/k/a Centre D'Etudes et Recherches Scientifique (Syria), Ministry of Defense (Syria), Lyongaksan Machineries and Equipment Export Corporation (North Korea), Changgwang Credit Corporation (North Korea) [Sanctions Expired]

July 29, 1993: Sanctions imposed on two entities but names of penalized entities withheld on grounds that publication would be "harmful to the national security of the United States." [**Federal Register**, July 29, 1993, p. 40685.]

August 24, 1993: Ministry of Aerospace Industry (China), Ministry of Defense (Pakistan) [Sanctions against Chinese entities waived November 1, 1994; Sanctions expired for Pakistani entity]

August 2, 1995: Sanctions imposed but names of penalized entities withheld on grounds that publication would be "harmful to the national security of the United States." [**Federal Register**, August 2, 1995, p. 39469.]

July 13, 1995: Sanctions imposed but names of penalized entities withheld on grounds that publication would be "harmful to the national security of the United States." [**Federal Register**, July 13, 1995, p. 36177.]

NUCLEAR SANCTIONS

A detailed list of cases in which sanctions have been imposed under U.S. nuclear non-proliferation laws is not readily available. A number of the most prominent episodes can be described, however.

In 1979, under a law known as the "Symington Amendment," the United States terminated economic and military aid to Pakistan because of its importation of uranium enrichment technology while refusing to accept International Atomic Energy Agency (IAEA) monitoring of all of its nuclear activities; similar sanctions were invoked against Pakistan at about this time, under the "Glenn Amendment," because of Pakistan's importation of reprocessing (plutonium separation) technology, while refusing to accept comprehensive IAEA monitoring. No sanctions were imposed against the seller entities. The sanctions triggered by the importation enrichment technology were waived by the enactment of special statutory provisions from 1982 until 1994, but are now in force. The sanctions triggered by the importation of reprocessing technology were waived indefinitely in 1982, under a provision of the Glenn Amendment—a step that was reaffirmed in 1988.

In January 1988, under a 1985 law known as the "Solarz Amendment," President Ronald Reagan determined that Pakistan had engaged in illicit exports from the United States that were intended for use in the manufacture of a nuclear explosive device. President Reagan, however, exercised a waiver provision in the law to prevent the termination of U.S. assistance that the finding would otherwise have been triggered.

Aid and arms sales to Pakistan were ultimately terminated in 1990, when President George Bush was unable to certify that Pakistan did "not possess a nuclear explosive device," a finding required by a 1985 law known as the Pressler Amendment. This ban was partially waived through legislation known as the "Brown Amendment" in 1995 to permit Pakistan to receive certain military equipment purchased for cash.

Throughout much of the 1980s, sanctions under the Symington and Glenn Amendments were enforced against Argentina and Brazil for their importation of enrichment and/or reprocessing technology. No sanctions were imposed against the selling entities.

EXPORT CONTROLS:
IS HARDWARE THE KEY TODAY?

YUZO MURAYAMA

COCOM VERSUS NON-PROLIFERATION[1]

In examining export-control regimes in the post–Cold War era, it is essential first to understand the differences between the Coordinating Committee on Multilateral Export Controls (COCOM) and non-proliferation-types of export controls.[2] (COCOM was dissolved in March 1995.)

COCOM was a rather simple system in terms of the number of participants. The number of countries that participated in export control was 17, and the number of targeted countries to which technology flow was restricted was 11. In comparison, the non-proliferation type of export control regime includes a larger number of participants. As of January 1995, the membership of the Nuclear Supply Group was 31 countries; of the Australia group, 28 countries; and of the Missile Technology Control Regime, 25 countries. The important point is that it is the intention of these regimes to increase the number of member countries to raise the effectiveness of their controls. What this means, however, is that monitoring and enforcement within the regimes will be more difficult due to potential conflicts of interest among a larger number of participants.

One of the main characteristics of COCOM was its "short list and high fence"; only high technologies that were not available in the Eastern bloc were restricted rigorously. Non-proliferation regimes, in contrast, are trying to control technology flow to Third World countries, in which the technology level is much lower than in the former Soviet Union. In addition, in the case of control of biological- and chemical-weapon-related technologies, we are trying to control a lower level of technology. This makes both the control list and the potential supplier list longer; thus it becomes more difficult to monitor the technology flow.

Sometime after World War II, important dual-use technologies were developed and emerged from the U.S. military sector. This was because R&D expenditures were targeted for military and space technology development, and the U.S. military sector actively acquired these new technologies. Because of their high prices, the commercial sector could not fully use the new dual-use technologies right after the war. However, after prices came down and as applications for these technologies widened, the commercial sector began to use them. This trend was enhanced by stagnant military R&D and acquisition expenditures in the 1970s, and more and more useful dual-use technologies have since then been developed in the commercial sector. This general trend of dual-use technology development has important implications for the economic effects of imposing export controls. As more military-relevant, dual-use technologies come out of the commercial sector, it becomes necessary to control these technologies for non-proliferation purposes. However, the cost of controlling these technologies keeps increasing. That is, if we control the technologies that are developed for commercial uses for the sake of non-proliferation, this can have severe repercussions on the commercial sector.

One of the advantages that COCOM possessed was the existence of strong ideological ties among its member countries. All of them understood the danger of transfering sensitive technology to the Eastern bloc, and this in turn made enforcement of technology control relatively easy; breaking the agreement became a costly behavior for the participants. A non-proliferation regime, on the other hand, does not share similar ideological ties. Although there seems to be a rough consensus on the undesirability of transfering sensitive technology to countries such as Iraq, Libya, and North Korea, there are wide discrepancies of judgment with respect to other countries. One of the main reasons is the lack of clear ideological differences between member countries and targeted countries, which makes it difficult to find a rationale for export control. Therefore, the lack of ideological ties makes it more difficult to reach agreements and easier to break the agreements even after they are reached.

Most of the countries of East Asia were outside the COCOM regime. However, as an increasing number of these countries experience dynamic economic growth and raise their technological capabilities, they should not be allowed to stay outside the export-control framework. Some of the countries have already started to obtain technological and manufacturing capabilities that could provide a component for the production of weapons of mass destruction. In addition, it is possible that some countries could decide to develop these weapons using their technological prowess if the security environment in the region should worsen. Therefore, in the near future, we should consider seriously how we can incorporate the rapidly developing East Asian countries into the export-control community. The task is not an easy one, however, since some of the difficult characteristics of forming non-proliferation export controls are especially applicable to these East Asian countries.

First, once we start to incorporate the East Asian countries, the number of members in the regime has to increase, making arrangements and their enforcement more difficult. The problem is an especially difficult one in the case of East Asian countries, since they have different technological characteristics, trade patterns, political systems, and security interests. To incorporate such different countries in the regimes will be a very challenging task.

Second, the countries in this region are extremely sensitive to factors that would impede their exports, since these provide a very important basis for their economic growth. Export controls are of course considered an impeding factor for exports; therefore countries try to avoid such measures unless strong reasons exist for applying them. This conflict is a very severe one, since dual-use technologies have increased in importance for export controls. It is these very technologies that most of the East Asian are trying to promote and they want to export products based on them to increase economic growth.

APPROACHING EXPORT CONTROLS IN EAST ASIA

We need to consider the specific environment surrounding East Asia in forming effective export-control regimes in this region. The following factors are the most important.

Role of Foreign Companies

American and Japanese companies especially have played a large role in the region's economic growth by providing the necessary capital and technology. Although some countries have raised their indigenous technological capability, foreign companies still play a significant role. As a result, while exports of high technology-related products keep increasing at a rapid pace, most of these are still being produced by subsidiaries of foreign companies located in East Asia. This is especially so in countries such as Malaysia and Singapore, which try to attract foreign high-tech companies.

The implication of this fact for export controls is that it is extremely important for foreign companies operating in East Asia that the same export-control measures be implemented in these countries as exist in their home countries. Although the role of foreign companies might decrease in time as East Asian countries develop greater indigenous capabilities, for now, it is one of the factors most significant for export controls in the region. In addition, it is important for foreign companies that export control measures be transferred through their relationships when they form joint ventures or business alliances with companies in the countries of this region. This kind of effort will have a positive long-run effect on the export-control environment in these countries.

A Checking System for Re-Exports

Countries such as Hong Kong and Singapore have become major world transshipment points. The same could be said about the role of East Asian countries as world manufacturing centers. These are the kinds of places where products move quickly from one country to another. In countries where this happens, concern exists that they could be used as transshipment points to conceal the final destination of sensitive items. It is necessary to establish a checking system for this kind of re-export of goods.

In establishing such a system, cooperation from the countries that have experience in export control and data on sensitive final users is essential. By providing and sharing various data on export control, we can start developing a meaningful checking system. Thus, in this respect, the role of the United States and Japan is significant as well.

A Flexible System

The countries in East Asia have fairly diverse political, economic, and trade characteristics. For instance, transshipment is the most important element for export control in Singapore, while the role of foreign companies is the essential element for export control in Malaysia, because of its economic policy of attracting foreign capital and technology. Similarly, international political conditions have to be taken into account when we consider export control in Taiwan.

It would be difficult as well as inefficient to apply one general rule of export control to all these countries in a short span of time. A better approach would be to make each country conform to international standards of export control gradually, as its indigenous technological level goes up, and to take into account each country's specific economic and other characteristics.

COMMUNITY BUILDING

In order to take this gradual approach, it is essential to build an export-control community in the region, to raise awareness of the problem, and to promote understanding of the necessity of export controls. This is especially important in this region, since the network of security dialogue is still limited. Export-control community building would also contribute to forming a common ideology on the undesirability of developing weapons of mass destruction.

The United States and Japan, both of which have extensive economic activities and interests in the region, should make efforts to cooperate in forming such an export-control community at both the governmental and non-governmental levels. Both countries possess the resources and interests to promote this kind of an initiative in East Asia.

Notes

[1] The author is currently working on issues related to export controls in East Asia with Richard Cupitt, Center for International Trade and Security, University of Georgia. This paper draws partially on the results of our joint research.

[2] For a detailed analysis on the differences between the COCOM and non-proliferation export controls, using the cartel theory, see Yuzo Marayama, "Dual-Use Technologies and Export Controls: An Economic Analysis," in Gary Bertsch, Richard Cupitt, and Takehiko Yamamoto, eds., U.S. and Japanese Nonproliferation Export Controls: Theory, Description and Analysis (Lanham, MD: University Press of America, 1995).

ACRONYMS

ABM	Anti-Ballistic Missile (Treaty)
ACSA	Acquisition and Cross-Servicing Agreement
APEC	Asia-Pacific Economic Cooperation
ASEAN	Association of Southeast Asian Nations
ASIATOM	Asian Atomic Energy Community
BMD	Ballistic Missile Defense
CBW	Chemical or Biological Weapon
CFE	Conventional Forces in Europe
CIS	Commonwealth of Independent States
CNNC	China National Nuclear Corporation
COCOM	Coordinating Committee on Multilateral Export Controls
CSCE	Conference on Security and Cooperation in Europe
CTBT	Comprehensive Test Ban Treaty
DPRK	Democratic People's Republic of Korea
DMZ	Demilitarized Zone
EAEC	East Asian Economic Cooperation
EURATOM	European Atomic Energy Community
FBR	fast-breeder reactor
HEU	highly enriched uranium
HWR	heavy-water reactor
IAEA	International Atomic Energy Agency
ICBM	intercontinental ballistic missile
INF	Intermediate Nuclear Forces (Treaty)
INFCE	International Nuclear Fuel Cycle Evaluation
KEDO	Korean Energy Development Organization
LNFZ	limited nuclear-free zone
LWR	light-water reactor
MFN	most-favored-nation
MIRV	multiple independency targetable re-entry vehicle
MIT	Ministry of International Trade and Industry
MOX	plutonium and uranium mixed oxide
MTCR	Missile Technology Control Regime
NAFTA	North American Free Trade Agreement
NASAP	Non-Proliferation Alternative Systems Assessment Program
NATO	North Atlantic Treaty Organization
NICs	newly industrializing countries
NPPA	Nuclear Proliferation Prevention Act
NPR	Nuclear Posture Review
NPT	Nuclear Non-Proliferation Treaty
NWFZ	nuclear-weapons-free zone
OECD	Organisation for Economic Co-operation and Development
PACATOM	Pacific Atomic Energy Community
PTBT	Partial Test Ban Treaty
SDF	Self Defense Forces
SDPJ	Social Democratic Party of Japan
SEANFZ	Southeast Asian Nuclear-Free Zone
SLBM	submarine-launched ballistic missile
SPNFZ	South Pacific Nuclear-Free Zone
STAR	Strategic Arms Reduction Treaty
THAAD	Theater High-Altitude Area Defense
TMD	Theater Missile Defense
WEU	Western European Union

GLOSSARY*

atomic bomb A bomb whose energy comes from the fission of uranium or plutonium.

blanket A layer of fertile material, such as uranium-238 or thorium-232, placed around the core of a reactor. During operation of the reactor, additional fissile material is produced in the blanket.

breakout Decision of a nation to end its compliance with nuclear arms control or nuclear safeguards treaties.

breeder reactor A nuclear reactor that produces somewhat more fissile material than it consumes. The fissile material is produced both in the reactor's core and when neutrons are captured in fertile material placed around the core (blanket). This process is known as breeding. Breeder reactors have not yet reached commercialization, although active research and development programs are being pursued by a number of countries.

CANDU (Canadian deuterium-uranium reactor.) The most widely used type of heavy-water reactor. The CANDU reactor uses natural uranium as a fuel and heavy water as a moderator and a coolant.

chain reaction The continuing process of nuclear fissioning in which the neutrons released from a fission trigger at least one other nuclear fission. In a nuclear weapon, an extremely rapid, multiplying chain reaction causes the explosive release of energy. In a reactor, the pace of the chain reaction is controlled to produce heat (in a power reactor) or large quantities of neutrons (in a research or production reactor).

coolant A substance circulated through a nuclear reactor to remove or transfer heat. The most common coolants are water and heavy water.

core The central portion of a nuclear reactor containing the fuel elements and, usually, the moderator. Also the central portion of a nuclear weapon containing highly enriched uranium or plutonium.

counter-proliferation Defined by the U.S. Defense Department as programs designed to prevent adversaries from acquiring or using weapons of mass destruction, primarily by demonstrating that such weapons will not confer a battlefield advantage against U.S. forces. Counter-proliferation also implicitly poses the threat of a preemptive strike to neutralize the production facilities and storage sites of weapons of mass destruction before the onset of hostilities.

critical mass The minimum amount of fissile material required to sustain a chain reaction. The exact mass varies with many factors such as the particular fissionable isotope present, its concentration and chemical form, the geometrical arrangement of the material, and its density. When fissionable materials are compressed by high explosives in implosion-type atomic weapons, the critical mass needed for a nuclear explosion is reduced.

enrichment The process of increasing the concentration of one isotope of a given element (in the case of uranium, increasing the concentration of uranium-235).

---

*Drawn and partly adapted, with permission, from glossary in Leonard S. Spector, Mark G. McDonough, with Evan S. Medeiros, *Tracking Nuclear Proliferation: A Guide in Maps and Charts, 1995* (Washington, D.C.: Carnegie Endowment for International Peace, 1995).

feed stock Material introduced into a facility for processing.

fission The process by which a neutron strikes a nucleus and splits it into fragments. During the process of nuclear fission, several neutrons are emitted at high speed, and heat and radiation are released.

fissile material Material composed of atoms which readily fission when struck by a neutron. Uranium-235 and plutonium-239 are examples of fissile materials.

fusion The formation of a heavier nucleus from two lighter ones (such as hydrogen isotopes), with the attendant release of energy (as in a hydrogen bomb).

gas centrifuge process A method of isotope separation in which heavy gaseous atoms or molecules are separated from light ones by centrifugal force.

gaseous diffusion A method of isotope separation based on the fact that gas atoms or molecules with different masses will diffuse through a porous barrier (or membrane) at different rates. The method is used to separate uranium-235 from uranium-238.

gas-graphite reactor A nuclear reactor in which a gas is the coolant and graphite is the moderator.

heavy water Water containing significantly more than the natural proportion (1 in 6,500) of heavy hydrogen (deuterium) atoms to ordinary hydrogen atoms. (Hydrogen atoms have one proton, deuterium atoms have one proton and one neutron.) Heavy water is used as a moderator in some reactors because it slows down neutrons effectively and does not absorb them (unlike light, or normal, water) making it possible to fission natural uranium and sustain a chain reaction.

heavy-water reactor A reactor that uses heavy water as its moderator. Depending on the reactor's design, this can permit the reactor to use natural uranium as fuel. See CANDU.

highly enriched uranium Uranium in which the percentage of uranium-235 nuclei has been increased from the natural level of 0.7 percent to some level greater than 20 percent, usually around 90 percent.

hydrogen bomb A nuclear weapon that derives its energy largely from fusion. Also known as a thermonuclear bomb.

kilogram (kg) A metric weight equivalent to 2.2 pounds.

kiloton (Kt) The energy of a nuclear explosion that is equivalent to an explosion of 1,000 tons of TNT.

laser enrichment method A still experimental process of uranium enrichment in which a finely tuned, high-power laser is used to differentially excite various uranium isotopes. This differential excitation makes it possible to separate uranium-235 from uranium-238.

light water Ordinary water (H_2O), as distinguished from heavy water (D_2O)

light-water reactor A reactor that uses ordinary water as moderator and coolant and low-enriched uranium as fuel.

low-enriched uranium Uranium in which the percentage of uranium-235 nuclei has been increased from the natural level of 0.7 percent to less than 20 percent, usually 3 to 6 percent. With the increased level of fissile material, low-enriched uranium can sustain a chain reaction when immersed in lightwater and is used as fuel in lightwater reactors.

megawatt (Mw) One million watts. Used in reference to a nuclear power plant, one million watts of electricity (Mwe); used in reference to a research or production reactor, one million watts of thermal energy (MWt).

metric ton One thousand kg. A metric weight equivalent to 2,200 pounds or 1.1 tons.

nuclear energy The energy liberated by a nuclear reaction (fission or fusion) or by spontaneous radioactivity.

nuclear fuel Basic chain-reacting material, including both fissile and fertile materials. Commonly used nuclear fuels are natural uranium and low-enriched uranium; high-enriched uranium and plutonium are used in some reactors.

nuclear fuel cycle The set of chemical and physical operations needed to prepare nuclear material for use in reactors and to dispose of or recycle the material after its removal from the reactor. Existing fuel cycles begin with uranium as the natural resource and create plutonium as a by-product. Some future fuel cycles may rely on thorium and produce the fissile isotope uranium-233.

nuclear fuel fabrication plant A facility where the nuclear material (e.g., enriched or natural uranium) is fabricated into fuel elements to be inserted into a reactor.

nuclear power plant Any device or assembly that converts nuclear energy into useful power. In a nuclear electric power plant, heat produced by a reactor is used to produce steam to drive a turbine that in turn drives an electricity generator.

nuclear reactor A device for the controlled use of nuclear energy for such purposes as the production of electricity, the production of isotopes, research, and propulsion. Reactors are of three general types: power reactors, production reactors, and research reactors.

nuclear waste The radioactive by-products formed by fission and other nuclear processes in a reactor. Most nuclear waste is initially contained spent fuel. If this material is reprocessed, new categories of waste result.

nuclear weapons A collective term for atomic bombs and hydrogen bombs. Weapons based on a nuclear explosion. Generally used throughout the text to mean atomic bombs only, unless used with reference to nuclear-weapon states (all five of which have both atomic and hydrogen weapons).

plutonium-239 (Pu239) A fissile isotope occurring naturally in only minute quantities, which is manufactured artificially when uranium-238, through irradiation, captures an extra neutron. It is one of the two materials that have been used for the core of nuclear weapons, the other being highly enriched uranium.

plutonium-240 (Pu249) A fissile isotope produced in reactors when a plutonium-239 atom absorbs a neutron instead of fissioning. Its presence complicates the construction of nuclear explosives because of its high rate of spontaneous fission.

power reactor A reactor designed to produce electricity as distinguished from reactors used primarily for research or for producing radiation or fissionable materials.

190

production reactor A reactor designed primarily for large-scale production of plutonium-239 by neutron irradiation of uranium-238.

radioactivity The spontaneous disintegration of an unstable atomic nucleus, resulting in the emission of subatomic particles.

recycle To reuse the remaining uranium and plutonium found in spent fuel after they have been separated at a reprocessing plant from unwanted radioactive waste products also in the spent fuel.

reprocessing Chemical treatment of spent reactor fuel to separate the plutonium and uranium from the unwanted radioactive waste by-products and (under present plans) from each other.

research reactor A reactor primarily designed to supply neutrons for experimental purposes. It may also be used for training, materials testing, and production of radioisotopes.

spent fuel Fuel elements that have been removed from the reactor after use because they contain too little fissile material and too high a concentration of unwanted radioactive by-products to sustain reactor operation. Spent fuel is both thermally and radioactively hot.

thermonuclear bomb A hydrogen bomb.

uranium A radioactive element with the atomic number 92 and, as found in natural ores, an average atomic weight of 238. The two principal natural isotopes are uranium-235 (0.7 percent of natural uranium), which is fissile, and uranium-238 (99.3 percent of natural uranium), which is fertile.

uranium-233 (U233) A fissile isotope bred in fertile thorium-232. Like plutonium-239, it is theoretically an excellent material for nuclear weapons, but is not known to have been used for this purpose. Can be used as reactor fuel.

uranium-235 (U235) The only naturally occurring fissile isotope. Natural uranium contains 0.7 percent U235; light-water reactors use about 3 percent and weapons grade, highly enriched uranium normally consists of 93 percent of this isotope.

uranium-238 (U238) A fertile material. Natural uranium is composed of approximately 99.3 percent U238.

weapons-grade Nuclear material of the type most suitable for nuclear weapons, i.e., uranium enriched to 93 percent U235 or plutonium that is primarily Pu~39.

weapons-usable Fissionable material that is weapons-grade or, though less than ideal for weapons, can still be used to make a nuclear explosive.

yellowcake A concentrate produced during the milling process that contains about 80 percent uranium oxide (U308). In preparation for uranium enrichment, the yellowcake is converted to uranium hexafluoride gas (UF6). In the preparation of natural uranium reactor fuel, yellowcake is processed into purified uranium dioxide. Sometimes uranium hexafluoride is produced as an intermediate step in the purification process.

yield The total energy released in a nuclear explosion. It is usually expressed in equivalent tons of TNT (the quantity of TNT required to produce a corresponding amount of energy).

191

THE CARNEGIE ENDOWMENT
FOR INTERNATIONAL PEACE

The Carnegie Endowment for International Peace was established in 1910 in Washington, D.C., with a gift from Andrew Carnegie. As a tax-exempt operating (not grant-making) foundation, the Endowment conducts programs of research, discussion, publication, and education in international affairs and U.S. foreign policy. The Endowment publishes the quarterly magazine, *Foreign Policy*.

Carnegie's senior associates—whose backgrounds include government, journalism, law, academia, and public affairs—bring to their work substantial first-hand experience in foreign policy. Through writing, public and media appearances, study groups, and conferences, Carnegie associates seek to invigorate and extend both expert and public discussion on a wide range of international issues, including worldwide migration, nuclear nonproliferation, regional conflicts, multilateralism, democracy-building, and the use of force. The Endowment also engages in and encourages projects designed to foster innovative contributions in international affairs.

In 1993, the Carnegie Endowment committed its resources to the establishment of a public policy research center in Moscow designed to promote intellectual collaboration among scholars and specialists in the United States, Russia, and other post-Soviet states. Together with the Endowment's associates in Washington, the center's staff of Russian and American specialists conduct programs on a broad range of major policy issues ranging from economic reform to civil-military relations. The Carnegie Moscow Center holds seminars, workshops, and study groups at which international participants from academia, government, journalism, the private sector, and nongovernmental institutions gather to exchange views. It also provides a forum for prominent international figures to present their views to informed Moscow audiences. Associates of the center also host seminars in Kiev on an equally broad set of topics.

The Endowment normally does not take institutional positions on public policy issues. It supports its activities principally from its own resources, supplemented by nongovernmental, philanthropic grants.

THE INTERNATIONAL HOUSE OF JAPAN

The International House of Japan is a private, non-profit organization incorporated in 1952, with support from the Rockefeller Foundation and other private institutions and individuals, for the purpose of promoting cultural exchange and intellectual cooperation between the peoples of Japan and those of other countries.

Housed in a handsome structure built in Tokyo in 1955 and enlarged in 1976, it is a working international community engaged directly in a variety of programs that embody the free exchange and interaction of ideas and that strive to foster a climate favorable to international cooperation.

The House program embraces a wide variety of projects. It sponsors the international exchange of individual leaders, scholars, and artists; cooperates with other organizations having similar goals and purposes; renders assistance to visiting individual scholars, researchers, and artists; arranges seminars, lecture meetings, conferences, and study groups; provides fellowships and scholarships; initiates and assists in research projects; publishes books and newsletters; and operates a selective library focusing on the study of modern Japan.

JAPAN'S NUCLEAR FUTURE:
THE PLUTONIUM DEBATE AND EAST ASIAN SECURITY

SELIG S. HARRISON, EDITOR

The Japanese decision to build independent plutonium reprocessing capabilities is officially explained in terms of national energy security and environmental priorities. In a 1971 resolution known as the Three Non-Nuclear Principles, the Japanese Diet pledged that Japan "will not manufacture or possess nuclear weapons." But neighboring East Asian countries, eyeing Japan's plutonium stockpiles and the sophisticated rocketry in its space program, are suspicious of Japanese intentions.

This book presents the views of a leading Japanese proponent of the reprocessing policy, Atsuyuki Suzuki, Professor of Nuclear Engineering at Tokyo University; a leading critic, Jinzaburo Takagi, Director of the Citizens Nuclear Information Center, and Taewoo Kim, Senior Researcher of the Peace Studies Research Institute in Seoul, who warns that the Japanese nuclear program could lead South Korea, or a unified Korea, to pursue comparable reprocessing capabilities.

Assessing the possibility of a nuclear-armed Japan, Selig S. Harrison, Director of the Carnegie Endowment Project on Japan's Role in International Security Affairs and former Northeast Asia Bureau Chief of the *Washington Post*, analyzes the domestic debate in Japan over nuclear policy and the factors that will determine whether or not Japan will become a nuclear-weapons power.

"The bottom line is that the continuance of the American nuclear umbrella over Japan will not, in itself, assure a non-nuclear Japan unless it is accompanied by meaningful U.S. and Russian steps leading to a global process of nuclear disarmament embracing China . . . In a world moving toward denuclearization, however gradually, Japan's anti-nuclear consensus is likely to hold firm. In a world with a frozen power structure dominated by five countries claiming the right to a perpetual nuclear monopoly, Japanese nationalism is likely to triumph, in the end, over the 'nuclear allergy.'"
—from the Overview by Selig S. Harrison

Order through Carnegie's distributor:
Brookings Institution Press, Tel. 1-800-275-1447 or 202-797-6258. Fax. 202-797-6004.
ISBN: 0-87003-065-5 $12.95